From the To

Stories and poems collected

John Seely
Frank Green
Graham Nutbrown

Oxford University Press   1989

Oxford University Press, Walton Street, Oxford OX2 6DP

Oxford New York Toronto
Delhi Bombay Calcutta Madras Karachi
Petaling Jaya Singapore Hong Kong Tokyo
Nairobi Dar es Salaam Cape Town
Melbourne Auckland

and associated companies in
Berlin Ibadan

Oxford is a trade mark of Oxford University Press

ISBN 0 19 831250 4

Phototypeset by Pentacor Limited, High Wycombe
Printed in Great Britain by The Alden Press, Oxford

Illustrations in text by Mick Armson, Jill Barton, Chris Duggan, Peter Elson, Clive Goodyer, Leo Hartas, Debbie Hinks, Angela McKay, Peter Melnyczuk, Colin Paine, Claire Pound, Chris Price, Tracey Ramsdale, Mark Rowney, John Tennent.

Cover illustration by Karen Jarman.

Contents

Acknowledgements

The editors and publishers are grateful for permission to include the following copyright material:

Isaac Asimov: 'The Fun They Had' from *Earth is Room Enough*. Copyright © 1957 by Isaac Asimov. Reprinted by permission of Doubleday a division of Bantam, Doubleday, Dell Publishing Group Inc. Guy Burt: 'Unsuspected Hero' from *Young Words*. Reprinted by permission of Macmillan Accounts and Administration Ltd. John Cunliffe: 'Alpha-B375—Earth Visitor's Guide' from *Standing on a Strawberry*, Reprinted by permission of Andre Deutsch Ltd. Eric Finney: 'Our Solar System' from *Spaceways* edited by John Foster (OUP 1986). Reprinted by permission of the author. Nicholas Fisk: 'Living Fire' from *Living Fire* Corgi & Bantam Books Ltd). © 1986 Nicholas Fisk. Reprinted by permission of Laura Cecil. Mick Gowar: 'An English Lesson', and 'Closing of the Door' both from *So Far So Good*, © Mick Gowar 1986. Reprinted by permission of William Collins Sons & Co. Ltd., Susan Gregory: 'S.H.C.' from *Martini-on-the-Rocks and Other Stories* (Kestrel Books, 1984), © Susan Gregory 1984, Reprinted by permission of Penguin Books Ltd. Julie Harrison: 'Secrets' from *Young Writers 26th Year*, (Heinemann Educational Books Ltd, 1985)** Clare Milner: 'The Escapologist' from *Young Words*. Reprinted by permission of Macmillan Accounts and Administration Ltd. Rita Morris: 'The Waiting Game' reprinted from *Space 9* (ed. R. Davis, Century Hutchinson 1985). Copyright the author.** Liam O'Flaherty: 'His first Flight' from *The Short Stories of Liam O'Flaherty*. Reprinted by permission of Jonathan Cape Ltd., on behalf of the Estate of Liam O'Flaherty: Michael Rosen: 'Going Through Old Photos' from *Quick Let's Get Out of Here,* Reprinted by permission of Andre Deutsch Ltd. Iain Crichton Smith: 'Do you believe in ghosts?'. Reprinted by permission of the author. Andrew Taylor: 'Running Away?' from *Win Some Lose Some* edited by Jo Goodman. (Fontana 1985)**

Every effort has been made to contact copyright holders before publication, however in some cases** this has not been possible. If contacted the publisher will ensure that full credit is given at the earliest opportunity.

How are you getting on at school?

In this section there are two stories and a poem about school. One of the stories comes from England, and the other one from Australia. They are all about relationships – how are *you* getting on at school?

S.H.C.

When Mrs Hopkins left to have a baby, One Set Two had a new teacher for English. The new teacher was soft and did a lot of grinning. You could tell her *anything*. They called her Smiler. She smiled on and on, even when they made a racket. One Set Two thought she wasn't quite right in the head.

On this particular morning, the boys came charging into Smiler's room before the girls, hot-foot from Registration. Some pulled up abruptly as they crashed across the threshold, as if an invisible rider had yanked hard on an imaginary rein. They looked across at Smiler. But she never said, 'Go out and form a line and do it *properly* this time.' She just smiled on.

'Miss, Miss!' yelled Gary Radford, flapping the air with *Adventures in Science*, Issue One. He was building it up into an encyclopædia. 'Will you read us a bit out of this? It's dead good – all about S.H.C.'

'S.H.C.?' smiled Smiler, raising an eyebrow and scratching her nose. 'What's S.H.C.?'

'Spontaneous Human Combustion. It says this man went up in flames when he was just sitting on the *bog*. It says it's caused by stress.'

The girls, who didn't charge through the door but appeared to sleepwalk in, leaning at an angle of forty-five degrees to the door jambs and one another, groaned heavily. 'Aw, Miss. Don't let them get on to S.H.C. It takes for ever.'

Three others had joined Gary, clamouring round Miss at the table, jabbing well-chewed fingers at the pictures. 'Look at *this*, Miss. Isn't it 'orrible?' 'Go on, read it, Miss.' 'Yeah, Miss! I've got this book all about S.H.C. at home, Miss. I'll bring it in tomorrer.'

'Mrs Walker!' A tall thin figure at the door. All eyes swivelled to it. The Deputy Headmistress, quivering like a compass needle.

'I don't think One Set Two has time to waste being read to, Mrs Walker. One Set Two cannot spell "cuneiform".

6

They cannot spell "Tutankhamun". One Set Two cannot even spell "pyramid" or "papyrus".' Flecks of spit flew before Mrs Cuthbert's words and she scanned the class, like a ship's beam, for gigglers. 'I thought, Mrs Walker, that you might outline the story of Antony and Cleopatra for them this morning. To assist them with their History. I am all in favour, One Set Two, of an integrated curriculum.' And with that she cruised off.

One Set Two looked a little stunned. 'She's all in favour of what-er?' asked Barbara Heyward.

'Summat to do with curry, weren't it?' said David Wheeler. 'Must be a Paki-lover.'

'Shurrup, you,' growled Baljit Singh, shoving David.

'Shurrup, yourself, Sing-a-Song-of-Sixpence,' said David, snatching Baljit's rubber and flicking it across to Peter Kilbourne who fielded it neatly.

'Mrs Cuthbert dictates History that fast,' grumbled Sharon Perkins, 'me arm feels like it's gonna drop off.'

'Well now,' said Mrs Walker, hitching her skirt and sitting on the edge of the table. 'Antony and Cleopatra. Cleopatra was an adventurous lady. She was once delivered to a man, rolled up in a carpet.'

One Set Two punched one another in delight and giggled and whispered behind their hands and settled down.

'Can we act it, Miss?' said Julie Hill who fancied being Cleopatra.

'Yeah,' said David Wheeler, turning his head till his nose was parallel with his shoulder and talking out of the side of his mouth. 'And you can be the carpet, baby.'

'Cleopatra put an asp to her busom,' wrote Gary Radford that evening in the exercise-book he used for a diary. 'An asp is a venomous serpent. She must've got *sucked* to death.' Gary looked thoughtfully at what he'd just written. This week he was practising writing very, very small. He was currently averaging twenty-two words to the line. The Deputy Head had written, 'This is the work of a demented ant', in big letters across his History book. He looked back at last week's entries. Last week he'd been into topping his 'i's and 'j's with little circles instead of dots, and the Deputy Head had written, 'Stop this affectation', and the week before that he'd done great looping 'g's and 'y's, heavy as pears, drooping on to the line below. He didn't have room for the words and had to squash them all up and even he'd got confused. The Deputy Head had written, 'Contracted the dropsy?' He didn't know what she was on about in any of them.

Gary turned his thoughts away from his handwriting and back to Cleopatra. How horrible to be sucked to death by a snake! No more horrible, though, than spontaneously to combust. Gary shifted in his chair and began to tear at the skin round his fingers with his teeth. Was there some warning when it was going to happen? Could you feel yourself hotting up? They say it's caused by stress. Gary was under a lot of stress at the moment. Apart from worrying that he might burst into flames at any moment, he was worried that Mrs Walker might not be teaching him English properly. His mam was dead set on him getting O-levels like his cousin Ian. Only another five years and he'd be taking them. He was also worried because everybody in his class had suddenly started fancying everybody else and all he wanted in life was a ferret. He felt very alone. He put a hand to his forehead. Pretty hot. He turned out the electric fire in his bedroom and went across to the bathroom to splash cold water on his face. That should cool him down. He pushed a lot of bottles and packets around in the bathroom cupboard looking for a thermometer. If his temperature was up, he'd take a cold bath . . .

When the boys came tearing into Mrs Walker's room the next day they showed her 'The Beckoning Lady' in *Adventures in Science*. It came under the section 'Apparitions, Poltergeists and E.S.P.' and told how a woman woke one night to see a ghost dressed in grey with an old-fashioned bonnet walk out of her wardrobe and stand by her bed. The ghost didn't *do* anything – just looked down on the woman without smiling. The same thing happened the next night. But the night after that the grey lady crossed to the window and beckoned. 'And I knew then,' said the woman, 'that what she wanted was to entice me to jump to my death.' She had every reason to think so, too, living on the thirty-third floor of a high-rise block. The girls, who loped into the room in the middle of Mrs Walker reading the story, shuddered and clutched each other. All except Julie Hill who was stuck in the doorway between a suitcase and what looked like a large roll of carpet.

'I had this dream once,' said Gary in a low voice to Mrs Walker as she waved the rest of the class to their places, 'that I was looking at my own tombstone.' He said it low because in point of fact he'd seen it on 'Strange Tales' on the telly. He didn't suppose Mrs Walker ever watched 'Strange Tales'. All teachers watch is the Last Night of the Proms and Party Political Broadcasts.

'Tutankhamun,' said Mrs Walker when at last they had settled down and were still, 'was a king and he died very young.' Gary began to feel himself hotting up. 'He married a child bride.' Gary felt himself getting yet hotter. 'The two of them were not much older than you lot. When he died he was only in his teens and they buried him in the Valley of the Kings. In a tomb of gold within a room of gold, with a gold chariot, and a death mask of gold upon his face. Can you imagine what it was like when they found the entrance to the tomb, only this century, and room after golden room?' One Set Two stirred. 'On top of his tomb,' said Mrs Walker, 'his bride placed a garland of flowers. Think how sad she must have been. The tomb was sealed up and the air was so still that the flowers remained intact for over three thousand years. But when they opened up the chamber, the air got in and the flowers just crumbled into dust.' One Set Two sighed and were still.

'Can we do Cleopatra now, Miss?' asked Julie Hill at last. 'I've brought a bit of carpet in, Miss,' and she yanked up the roll from the gangway to show Mrs Walker.

'All right,' said Mrs Walker, 'but just let's go over the story once again. If you remember, Antony was Cleopatra's boy-friend much later than the carpet incident. Who was Cleopatra's boy-friend earlier on, when she was delivered all rolled up?'

Gary's hand shot up. A look of intense pain came over his face, as he gripped his armpit with his other hand and flicked from the wrist as if he wanted shut of his fingers for ever. 'Miss. Oooh, Miss.'

'Yes, Gary.'

'Caesar, Miss,' said Gary crisply, looking triumphantly round at the others as if expecting a standing ovation. Julie Hill pulled her eyes down at the corners at him till the reds showed.

'Quite right, Gary,' said Mrs Walker, 'and since you show such enthusiasm, I think you should play the part of Caesar, don't you?'

The class cheered and Gary buckled up. '*Oh, no*, Miss. Please.' Julie Hill squealed in distress, rolled down her lower lip and dashed her face into her hands, but very soon recovered. 'I've brought a costume as well, Miss,' she said, now hoisting up the suitcase. 'Can I go to the toilets to change?'

Mrs Walker gave permission and Julie, hardly able to believe her luck, said quickly, 'Can Sharon come too, Miss, to help me get ready?' She stuck up both thumbs and nodded her head very fast at her friend like a chicken

pecking corn. The two of them dashed out, leaving the class to dream up suitable clothing for Imperial Caesar.

Fifteen minutes later Julie and Sharon returned, bent double with laughing, holding one another up. Cleopatra wore her coat clutched round her middle like a dressing-gown and from underneath floated a lot of shocking pink net. Her eyes had been alarmingly extended towards her eyebrows with bat wings of blue paint and edged with wiggly black lines. Her lips were plastered thick as raspberry jam on toast. She wore a gold head-band slung low across her brow from which sprouted a peacock feather so long it bent as she entered the door. Across her forehead, cheeks and chin she had stuck pink and purple sequins and she jangled at the wrist and ankle with lines and lines of bracelets, and row upon row of beads clinked against the studs of what looked like a dog-collar round her neck. She waded into the room on four-inch stiletto mules.

Four handmaidens and four carpet-bearers were sent off to wrap up the human parcel and at last the carpet was carried shoulder high from the jumping horse just outside the door with Julie Hill ceremonially rolled up inside it. Or, rather, her head and body were rolled up but her legs stuck out at the other end like a mummified clothes-peg.

11

With a jerk and a bump the package was placed on the ground at the feet of Imperial Caesar who wore five tea towels borrowed from the Home Economics block for a toga. Two round his legs, two round his body and one draped becomingly over one shoulder. On his head he wore a crown of wire with a few browning ivy leaves growing out of it. Baljit Singh, who was the carpet-seller, said, 'I have a fine piece from the East for your delight, O Caesar,' and with a flourish unrolled the carpet with his foot. Up jumped Julie Hill, hair and eyes wild, cheeks red as crabapples, and Caesar the Great choked and clutched himself with horror as a great wave of blistering heat broke over him at the sight of her, and the Deputy Head walked in.

What the Deputy Head saw was One Set Two jumping up and down in the gangways. One Set Two kneeling on desks, One Set Two gasping for breath and clinging on to one another and generally falling about. That terrible Julie Hill was leaping up like a Hollywood star out of a birthday cake, wearing what looked like her mother's negligee and an awful lot of jewellery and little else besides. And Gary Radford was dressed entirely in tea towels with *ivy leaves* in his hair and was clearly over-excited.

'*Mrs Walker!*' bellowed the Deputy Head. All eyes rushed to her, iron filings to a magnet. 'Can I have a word with you, please, *outside*.' Gary completely forgot that he was about to combust spontaneously in the delighted realisation that if anybody was going to, it would be the Deputy Head. She was as blotchy as salami and turning purple fast.

But when the Deputy Head returned five minutes later there was no sign of scorch marks, worse luck. She rapidly put an end to five glorious minutes during which One Set Two had run entirely amok. Cleopatra had married Caesar under a deluge of English exercise-book confetti and the happy couple were still sparkle-eyed and clutching hands. Four more girls had laid claim to four more boys by leaping out at them from a series of carpet packages and there was just about to be a mass wedding and another great confetti storm when the Deputy Head walked in for the second time.

Slowly, very slowly, like those suffering from hangovers after the most tremendous night on the town, One Set Two gathered up every scrap of confetti. The Deputy Head yanked Julie off to the cloakroom and personally supervised, arms crossed, while she scrubbed off every bit of the bat wings and the raspberry jam. Then she confiscated the magic carpet. 'Mrs Walker will no longer be taking you for English, One Set Two,' concluded the Deputy Head. 'I shall take that little responsibility entirely upon my own shoulders and from now on this period on a Friday will be given up entirely to a *Spelling Test!*'

But Gary hardly heard. Since he hadn't spontaneously combusted, that searing blast of heat could mean only one thing. *He actually fancied Julie Hill and he wasn't a freak after all.* And she'd married him in the face of Mrs Walker and an entire congregation.

Julie and Gary sat on the wall by the bus-stop after school with their arms round one another. Gary didn't remove his arm even when Mrs Walker grinned into view. He looked at her curiously instead for any signs of albino rabbit-pink eyes but she didn't look in the slightest put out. In fact she just carried straight on grinning. 'Have a good week-end, both of you,' she said, 'and don't go up in smoke.'

Gary grinned politely at her. 'No, we won't,' he said, and pulled Julie off the wall, keeping hold of her hand and whistling, as the bus came. No danger of that any longer, now he felt so grown-up and cool. He wasn't under any stress now, either, since they wouldn't be having Smiler for English. He was really glad about that. What with having the Deputy Head for Spelling every Friday, a whole galaxy of O-levels was positively guaranteed. He'd show his mam. He'd do just as good at school as his cousin Ian. And no sweat.

Susan Gregory

An English lesson

I

She daydreams:
A Lamborghini or a TR6 —
the coast road down to Monte Carlo or Loret.
The matching Gucci luggage in the boot;
my hand rests lightly on his neck.
His perfect suntanned features gleam,
his perfect pearl white teeth are set
in rugged concentration as — with perfect skill —
we purr down to his private beach
at Monte Carlo or Loret.

The snow lies crisp beneath the horses' hooves
and all the sleigh-bells ring as we ride back —
up to his family chateau in the Alps.
He won the giant slalom while I clapped and clapped
    and clapped.
His perfect suntanned features gleam,
his perfect pearl white teeth are set
in rugged concentration as — with perfect skill —
we glide on through the snow. His castle towers gleam
like wedding cake with frosted icing capped.

And in our paradise of love,
he sweeps me gently from my feet,
he holds me in his fine strong arms and
covers me with countless kisses sweet.

His perfect suntanned features gleam,
his perfect pearl white teeth are set
in perfect concentration – as with perfect skill –
he makes the earth move time and time again
like pounding waves beneath my trembling feet.

II

He writes, then thinks:
My eggs and bacon cooked the way I like –
the bacon crisp and crackling underneath the fork,
the hot fat spooned across the white.

The River Orwell at the crack of dawn –
the shadows long and sunlight sparkling fresh,
the first fat roaches nuzzling the bait.

Wembley: in extra time and still no score –
a long ball arcing through the biting air
splits the defence – the full-back high and dry,

the chip inside: I hit the perfect volley
on the turn . . . a micro-second's silence
smashed as 50,000 fans go wild.

(That looks all right.
The truth is,
if I had all that
I'd give it all for
just one
smile
from
Her.)

Mick Gowar

15

Running away?

Dear me,

It's me writing, I've been a bad boy. For a reward they're letting me use this typewriter for journal writing. Journal writing is just another word for diary. Diary is just another word for boring English work.

But at least it's not corrected and the teacher isn't allowed to read it. It's private.

I hate school. I hate school. I hate school. I hate school. I hate school. I hate school.

I can type anything I want. When I finish this I'll stick it in my journal file with all the other bits they've made me write. We do this twice a week. Our teacher is hard up for ideas.

October 24

Dear diary,

It's me again. I'm still using the typewriter. The teacher reckons they were happy with the amount I wrote (or really typed) last time, so I'm allowed to type again today.

But I'm not getting sucked in. I'm not writing any more than I want to. And I'm not getting sucked in to staying at school either just because they let me use the typewriter and the other kids have to handwrite their journals.

As soon as I'm ready, I'm running away again.

Last time was great (mostly) and now we know how to do it properly.

School sucks. Teachers are cops. But they can't read this – journals are absolutely private. Filed away till we next get to write in them. No one can read this but me. School sucks. School SUCKS!

October 28

Dear journal,

You're really a diary, but a snob name like journal might make you feel more important. (I don't think you are.)

I suppose you want to know why I ran away?

Well . . . answer, you dumb book.

I ran away because the whole school is like you. No one really cares. We just do stupid work that doesn't matter, then the bell rings, and we go to another room with another teacher and do more stupid work that doesn't matter.

When we've done that six times a day, they open the cages and we're free to do interesting things. Like earn some money selling papers, or go to footy training, or go to the video shop, or go to some kid's place and play video games, or anything that's better than school.

Plus, everyone picks on you. You get into trouble for really basic things like forgetting what your next class is and getting there late, or bringing the wrong books, or talking to someone, or messing up your page and not making it pretty like adults think they used to do. (How would they know? I've never seen them doing this work. It's all different to what they did anyway.)

I've written too much. I'm stopping.

Dear piece of paper,

Does this hurt you when the keys hit you? Do you feel like you're pushed around like we are?

I've just rolled you on a few lines. I've also typed a line of spaces and backspaces then hit the carriage return. I did it so you wouldn't feel the keys for a few minutes. But now the teacher is giving me dirty looks and thinks I'm just mucking around. So, sorry, but I've got to write again.

Running away. How did it start? Easy . . . we planned it for weeks. There was a show on TV about Ayer's Rock. That's about 2000 kilometres from Melbourne. It has a camping ground and you can climb the rock, the biggest in the world, about 348 metres high. It's pretty big, almost 9 kilometres around its base too.

We decided to go there next time one of us got into trouble. But first we had a few plans to make. I nicked a map at the petrol station and we worked out the best way to hitchhike there. To Adelaide is about 660 kilometres. We could do that in a night. Then it's another 1400 kilometres north. Once we got out of Adelaide we would probably get there in one ride, some road train going to Darwin would take us. (You go left before Alice Springs and hope for a tourist with a bit of space.)

For money we started saving our lunch money each day. For three weeks we pinched or borrowed from different teachers to buy our lunch. We each get a dollar a day for lunch, so in three weeks we had $15 each. We weren't too worried about paying back all the teachers, we'd never see them again.

We packed some bags with some clothes, our video games, and a few other things like a bit of food and stashed them in our hideout down one of the lanes. It meant we got hassled a bit for the money we borrowed and for not having our bags but it was worth it. We'd soon be free and no one could bug us ever again.

Time's up. Perk-u-later.

You slimy bastard. You miserable sneaking mongrel.
These journals are supposed to be private.
I know you've been reading this.
I'm finished.

You won't admit it will you? But I notice you watching me. And you're too chicken to admit that our journals aren't safe.

Who have you shown it to? My counsellor? The whole staffroom? Haven't you got anything to say?

Sorry

Dear slime,

At least you admit it. But there's nothing you can do about what I write in here because it's private. I haven't told anyone except Simon that you have read this yet. And he's going to be careful too from now on. But I could tell all the other kids that you sneak-read our journals when we've gone instead of just locking them up. We could organize every parent to complain to the Principal. You know how he hates parent complaints. You wouldn't stand a chance. He wouldn't listen to you. He just sucks up to the parents.

Why did you read it? Is spying something they teach you at college? And you wonder why kids don't trust teachers.

Sorry, again. You don't have to believe it, but it started as an accident. I dropped your file and the pages went everywhere. I started to put them back in order and accidentally read a bit. Then I read the lot. I liked it. You don't have to tell the other kids. I haven't read theirs. Can I read yours some more?

Dear diary (and others),

Look . . . I date my work. That way you'll be able to sort it more easily next time you drop it.

Why don't you date yours? Practise what you teach.

No, you can't read my diary. But you are anyway, aren't you?

You can't stop yourself, can you? I said 'NO', and you're still reading. Stop! Stop! Stop!

Are you still there?

I thought so.

OK, I quit. You win. Yes, you can read my journal. (Journal is a teachers'-college word for diary.)

November 14

Thanks.

November 18

Is that all?

We're supposed to write heaps and you just write one word.

Practise what you teach.

Did you ever run away?

1234567890-qwertyuiopasdfghjkl;:zxcvbnm,./
!"#$%&'()?≃QWERTYUIOPASDFGHJKL
+*ZXCVBNM◇?

See – I can pretend to be busy too.

November 18

Dear Edward (and diary),

OK . . . I'll write some more. Yes, I ran away once, when I was 13. I wasn't allowed to go out with my friends at the weekend so I took a bag of clothes and food and went down to the Yarra with my dog. The river was great but I started having second thoughts when it got dark.

I panicked, packed up and started walking home. (I didn't have enough money for a tram fare.) Then it started raining. I hid the bag in the garage when I got home and

then got yelled at for being out late in the wet. I was sent to
my room to do my homework without any dinner.
*   I still don't know if my parents realised I had run away.*
*   Your effort was a bit better. Tell me more sometime.*
*   But first, how did you know I had read your journal?*

Dear staff,
It's easy. But this bit is really confidential. The other kids
would kill me if they knew you knew.

There's heaps of ways to check.

Some kids tuck a bit of fluff or hair in their file then
check if it's been moved next time they get it from your
cupboard. Some dog-ear the corner of a page, because
teachers can't resist straightening out a creased page. Some
who are really game for a showdown write obscenities
about the teacher, or mention that they know who's letting
the teacher's tyres down.

The teachers can't resist following it up, even though
they weren't meant to read it. Your first reply is: 'But my
journal is private. You can't have read it. I trusted you!'
The teacher makes some excuse about national security.
Then you just deny you know anything about whatever
was written, and ask to see it. The teacher gets your
journal and you prove it isn't your handwriting. (The
teacher doesn't realize that you could have printed it left-
handed.) You're safe. They can't prove a thing.

My way is simple and not exactly foolproof, although it
did catch you. My work is on loose sheets, held together
with a paper clip; I always put one sheet in upside down. If
anyone reads it, they'll probably turn the page around for
me. Anyway, that's how I used to do it. I have a few other
methods up my sleeve too. Not that I need them, now that
you've confessed.

THIS ARTICLE IS COPYRIGHT, 1985
(So there!)

Dear Edward,

That's clever. Your secrets are safe with me. (I can already imagine your reaction to that line! 'Big deal!' or maybe something less printable.)

Actually I was impressed with some of the ways. We didn't do that stuff at school. Journals hadn't been invented then. In fact (you won't believe this but . . .) our work was even more boring than what you do now. We had no choice; we just wrote what the teacher told us.

How did you 'escape' from school when you ran away? One minute you were there, the next everyone was looking for you. They said you were heading for Ayer's rock.

November 25

Dear fans,

Easy. We had been planning the break-out for a while. We both had money stashed at home. But the eventual shoot-through happened a bit suddenly. It started when Simon turned off the main gas tap, so all the science rooms had no gas. The teacher accused him of sneaking up the front and getting at the tap (under her desk). Simon said he didn't do it but no one believed him as usual.

He was sent to the Vice Principal's office and told he was suspended for the day. He sent me a message. It was nearly recess. I knew what he wanted me to do. When he got the key to the bike shed we'd both get our bikes out before taking the key back to the office. We didn't figure that the VP would actually leave his office and open the bike shed personally. So when he'd gone, I climbed over the fence and passed my bike back over to Simon.

We could've taken 50 bikes if we'd wanted to.

Then we rode out of the yard and everyone knew we were going to Ayer's Rock. But when we went to Simon's place to get the money and food, his mum was still home. We went to my place and mum had gone out and locked it up. We got no more money – we only had our lunch money for that day.

So we rode to the station and got the train to the city,

then back out to Sandringham. That was the end of our lunch money. We were broke and it wasn't even lunchtime. We rode a bit down the coast to Black Rock and stopped for a swim. No one would think of looking for us at Black Rock. It was in the wrong direction, and 1980 kilometres closer to Melbourne than the other place. If they were looking for us, they had no hope. (Unfortunately, in all the rush of leaving earlier than we'd planned, we'd also forgotten to collect the bags we'd packed and left at our hideout.)

November 25

Dear Edward,
You're right. We didn't know where to look. To be honest, we didn't really think you'd get to Ayer's Rock, but we thought you might at least head west.

So now you were broke, penniless, and it wasn't even lunchtime. How did you manage? You didn't even have any food with you. (You always buy your lunch, don't you?)

November 28

Dear interrogator,
Don't you know how to survive in the big city? Or even the suburbs? You live off the land. Well, cars really. Half of them aren't locked and heaps of people leave loose change on the dash. Black Rock was as good as any other area we'd worked.

We had a simple code. 'Spotted' 'Check' 'Open' 'Watch' 'Move out'. When one of us said one of the code words, the other one knew what to do. We went through the shopping centre in about half an hour and had fifteen dollars.

Enough for a week.

This is a bit confidential. Like if anyone finds out about it, I'll say I didn't write it. Someone else must have borrowed the typewriter and typed this page and stuck it in my journal file. You can't prove a thing.

P.S. We don't do it any more. We got caught.

Dear Edward,

You crook! If anyone asks me if I knew you did that, I'll deny it too. I didn't write this. Some other teacher must have borrowed my typewriter and put this in your journal file for you to read.

I don't want to be an accomplice, an accessory after the fact.

But I'm glad you don't do it anymore. I'd hate to see you both go to Children's Court. You were lucky with whoever caught you – I guess they didn't call the police.

So what else did you do after arriving at Black Rock?

Dear co-conspirator,

I guess you did something like that too when you were young. You seemed too understanding to be a teacher. How come you didn't make a big deal out of it? Is this journal really confidential?

What do you think we did? What else do you do at the beach? We went for a swim. We didn't have our bathers so we rolled up our jeans and mucked around in the shallow water for a bit, then decided we didn't give damn so we dived in, clothes and all.

We figured we'd soon dry off, but it was colder than we thought. We were freezing when we got out of the water, so we went back into the bushes on the foreshore and made a circle out of some rocks and lit a fire. We hung our shirts on a tree hanging over the fire to dry them then went tearing round the park on our bikes to keep warm.

We found a big concrete pipe that you could ride through. Above that was this ace hill with a really steep drop at the end. When you rode down it you hit the beach at the bottom. Your front wheel dug into the sand and you flipped over the handlebars. We kept doing it till Simon hurt his shoulder. Then we got some pieces of wood and slid down on them.

When we got back to the fire, my shirt had slipped off the tree. Half of it was burned. I put it on anyway.

That was the bell for the end of the period. You'll have

to wait till the next journal day for the next exciting episode. Suffer!

December 2

Dear Edward,
So you've spent the day messing around on the beach, playing in the park, and other things like that. And I know now that you had some money for food, but what did you do about sleeping? You didn't have any sleeping-bags or blankets, did you?

December 5

Dear Persistent,
Are you getting paid for this or something? (I suppose you are, aren't you, or do teachers do this for cheap thrills?) OK, I'll tell you more.

TIME: 7 pm.
SCENE: Black Rock beach
MENU: Fish and Chips

Suddenly we heard a guy coming with a dog. We stashed the rest of the chips in the fork of a tree, where the dog couldn't reach it. Then we rolled over quietly and curled up in a big bush. The dog came right up to the bush and stuck his head in. He almost licked our faces, or he could have been trying to bite our heads off. But the guy yelled at the dog: 'Get out of there!'

We decided he might know we were there and be going to get the cops. So we grabbed our stuff and rode back to the shops. We got a bottle of Coke and a pack of smokes and went back to the big pipe. We lay in there with our schoolbags as pillows and had supper. Suddenly a cop car drove into the park. They stopped near the pipe with their lights shining right inside. We just lay flat and held our breath. They were looking right at us and they didn't even see us.

When they moved off, we decided we'd better find a new place too. We went back to the beach and moved along a bit further in case the guy with the dog came back. Suddenly, Simon screamed out. He'd walked right into a huge spider web, with a huge spider right in the middle of

25

it. Luckily he was pushing his bike, or he would have met the spider on his face.

We decided we didn't like the beach so much and went back to the shops again. They were all closed and so was the petrol station at the corner. But round the back was one of those Brotherhood bins where people leave their old clothes for poor people.

We decided that we were poor (we were cold anyway) and climbed inside. It was really small but we fitted. With the flap shut we would be dry if it rained. But we couldn't see outside and we wouldn't know when it was light. We didn't want to be still in the bin when the owner came to open the petrol station in the morning. I kept waking every half hour and asking Simon what time it was.

Eventually we both got used to being so cramped and sleeping crouched up vertically. When we woke up it was 8 o'clock in the morning. I guess the owner had slept in too, because we didn't see him.

Then we got on our bikes and started riding home. After about an hour we were starving again so we bought some doughnuts and a bottle of Coke.

December 5

Dear Edward,

I guess I'm writing short again. Flat out with correcting the senior essays and exams for their final results.

But I'm still reading and still interested. It's a real change to read something interesting each week or even twice a week.

Yeah . . . so what happened next?

December 9

Dear teach.,

Simple. We knew teachers didn't talk to each other much about what was happening around the place.

We arrived back at school five minutes after everyone had gone in from recess. We just went to our next class and

26

the teacher said: 'You're late! I hope you two have a good excuse.'

We did but he didn't bother to ask what it was.

THE END

December 9

Dear Edward,

You're kidding! I'll stir him when I see him next.

On a serious, final note ... thanks for some great reading. Thanks for letting me share some great writing.

Another year finished! Where did it go?

Have a great holiday!

December 12

You're welcome.

Have a great holiday too.

THE END AGAIN

December 16

You probably won't read this, but it doesn't matter. (Journals are private, of course.) Thanks, sort of, for 'making' me write. I think I'll do some more next year.

THE REAL END

Andrew Taylor

Thinking and writing

S.H.C. by Susan Gregory

This story comes from a collection called *Martini-on-the-Rocks*. There is also another collection of stories by Susan Gregory, called *Kill-a-Louse Week and Other Stories*.

There are three main characters in this story:
two teachers – Mrs Walker ('Smiler')
The Deputy Headmistress
and one pupil – Gary Radford. What impression do you get of each of them? What gives you this impression?

The writer uses some very vivid *comparisons* in the story, to help the reader imagine what she is trying to describe. For example, she describes the deputy headmistress as 'quivering like a compass needle'. This tells us not only that she is moving in a particular way but also that, like a compass needle, her body is pointing – towards where all the noise is coming from. Can you find any other comparisons that you think are very vivid?

An English lesson by Mick Gowar

Most people daydream sometimes. Sometimes the daydreams are caused by something that has happened in the real world. Stories about this include *The Secret Life of Walter Mitty* by James Thurber and *Billy Liar* by Keith Waterhouse.

Daydreaming is a good subject for your own stories or poems. Think of something in everyday life that can lead to a really vivid daydream – it could be something at school, or outside – and think of the possible results of daydreaming. Then write a story or a poem in which the daydream and the real world are mixed up together in some way.

Running away? by Andrew Taylor

Have you ever kept a diary or journal as part of your work in English?

If so, what agreement did you have with your teacher about what you wrote?

What was the point of the agreement?

What do you think about the way that Edward wrote in his journal?

What do you think of what his teacher did?

Try writing you own story about school and relationships. You could choose your own topic and title, or use one of these:

Teacher's pet hate
Running away
I tell you it won't happen again
School strike

That takes courage

In this section there are three stories and two poems about different aspects of courage. Are you afraid of branching out in life on your own, or of the dark, or of ghosts, or of . . . what? Whatever it is, there are some aspects of everybody's life that demand courage.

His first flight

The young seagull was alone on his ledge. His two brothers and his sister had already flown away the day before. He had been afraid to fly with them. Somehow when he had taken a little run forward to the brink of the ledge and attempted to flap his wings he became afraid. The great expanse of sea stretched down beneath, and it was such a long way down – miles down. He felt certain that his wings would never support him, so he bent his head and ran away back to the little hole under the ledge where he slept at night. Even when each of his brothers and his little sister, whose wings were far shorter than his own, ran to the brink, flapped their wings, and flew away he failed to muster up courage to take that plunge which appeared to him so desperate. His father and mother had come around calling to him shrilly, upbraiding him, threatening to let him starve on his ledge unless he flew away. But for the life of him he could not move.

That was twenty-four hours ago. Since then nobody had come near him. The day before, all day long, he had watched his parents flying about with his brothers and sister, perfecting them in the art of flight, teaching them how to skim the waves and how to dive for fish. He had, in fact, seen his older brother catch his first herring and devour it, standing on a rock, while his parents circled around raising a proud cackle. And all the morning the whole family had walked about on the big plateau midway down the opposite cliff, taunting him with his cowardice.

The sun was now ascending the sky, blazing warmly on his ledge that faced the south. He felt the heat because he had not eaten since the previous nightfall. Then he had found a dried piece of mackerel's tail at the far end of his ledge. Now there was not a single scrap of food left. He had searched every inch, rooting among the rough, dirt-caked straw nest where he and his brothers and sister had been hatched. He even gnawed at the dried pieces of spotted eggshell. It was like eating part of himself. He had then trotted back and forth from one end of the ledge to

the other, his grey body the colour of the cliff, his long grey legs stepping daintily, trying to find some means of reaching his parents without having to fly. But on each side of him the ledge ended in a sheer fall of precipice, with the sea beneath. And between him and his parents there was a deep, wide chasm. Surely he could reach them without flying if he could only move northwards along the cliff face? But then on what could he walk? There was no ledge, and he was not a fly. And above him he could see nothing. The precipice was sheer, and the top of it was perhaps farther away than the sea beneath him.

He stepped slowly out to the brink of the ledge, and, standing on one leg with the other leg hidden under his wing, he closed one eye, and then the other, and pretended to be falling asleep. Still they took no notice of him. He saw his two brothers and his sister lying on the plateau dozing, with their heads sunk into their necks. His father was preening the feathers on his white back. Only his mother was looking at him. She was standing on a little high hump on the plateau, her white breast thrust forward. Now and again she tore at a piece of fish that lay at her feet, and then scraped each side of her beak on the rock. The sight of the food maddened him. How he loved to tear food that way, scraping his beak now and again to whet it! He uttered a low cackle. His mother cackled too, and looked over at him.

'Ga, ga, ga,' he cried, begging her to bring him over some food. 'Gaw-ool-ah,' she screamed back derisively. But he kept calling plaintively, and after a minute or so he uttered a joyful scream. His mother had picked up a piece of the fish and was flying across to him with it. He leaned out eagerly, tapping the rock with his feet, trying to get nearer to her as she flew across. But when she was just opposite to him, abreast of the ledge, she halted, her legs hanging limp, her wings motionless, the piece of fish in her beak almost within reach of his beak. He waited a moment in surprise, wondering why she did not come nearer, and

then, maddened by hunger, he dived at the fish. With a loud scream he fell outward and downwards into space. His mother had swooped upwards. As he passed beneath her he heard the swish of her wings. Then a monstrous terror seized him and his heart stood still. He could hear nothing. But it only lasted a moment. The next moment he felt his wings spread outwards. The wind rushed against his breast feathers, then under his stomach and against his wings. He could feel the tips of his wings cutting through the air. He was not falling headlong now. He was soaring gradually downwards and outwards. He was no longer afraid. He just felt a bit dizzy. Then he flapped his wings once and he soared upwards. He uttered a joyous scream and flapped them again. He soared higher. He raised his breast and banked against the wind. 'Ga, ga, ga. Ga, ga, ga. Gaw-ool-ah.' His mother swooped past him, her wings making a loud noise. He answered her with another scream. Then his father flew over him screaming. Then he saw his two brothers and his sister flying around him curveting and banking and soaring and diving.

Then he completely forgot that he had not always been able to fly, and commenced himself to dive and soar and curvet, shrieking shrilly.

He was near the sea now, flying straight over it, facing straight out over the ocean. He saw a vast green sea beneath him, with little ridges moving over it, and he turned his beak sideways and crowed amusedly. His parents and his brothers and sister had landed on this green floor in front of him. They were beckoning to him, calling shrilly. He dropped his legs to stand on the green sea. His legs sank into it. He screamed with fright and attempted to rise again, flapping his wings. But he was tired and weak with hunger and he could not rise, exhausted by the strange exercise. His feet sank into the green sea, and then his belly touched it and he sank no farther. He was floating on it. And around him his family was screaming, praising him, and their beaks were offering him scraps of dog-fish.

He had made his first flight.

Liam O'Flaherty

Unsuspected hero

I really can't think of anyone whom I would like to be less than Jossy Pherit. To begin with, what about the name? And his dad – oh yes, his dad! Apart from providing employment for the constabulary, he was of no use to the community.

Even so, I like Jossy. He is one of nature's bad examples; a warning to humankind. He was quite illiterate. He went to school once – not that that proves anything though. Anyway, it all happened when we were fishing.

I'd got hold of the boat; the one Andy used to moor up by the Old Huts. We often went up by the Old Huts – there were good fish in the river there. The boat was just watertight and it was this relic we made use of on our fishing excursions.

Joss turned up late, with such a set of tackle you wouldn't see on a trout stream in the highlands. Green, it was; dark green, with little black rings and gauges and handles sprouting from it.

'Where in heaven did you get that?' asked the third member of our group, enviously. He was a young and inexperienced boy, who had been lumbered on us by his mother. 'Do take little Theodore with you, boy,' you know.

Jossy looked proud, and said nothing. And so we set out.

The boat took in some water, but it held together. Fishing was bad; even Jossy's real triple-hook-spinner didn't catch anything. Looking at him he was a strange sight; long, grainy black hair, and a wild light in his eyes. Subdued, though: that came from having a father like a sledgehammer.

He never did a thing right in his life. You name it, Jossy Pherit couldn't do it. Oh, except swim.

He could swim. Well, it came naturally – he learned at an early age that the only way to escape when thrown into the river is to swim across to the other side and go home.

'Hey look, blackb'ries!' yelled Joss. When I looked, sure enough there was a bush – no, two bushes – both laden.

'Stop the boat!' I cried, poling us frantically towards the bank.

'I want to fish,' said Ted, sullenly.

'I want blackb'ries,' said Jossy. I agreed.

'You stay here and fish,' we said. He did.

Those blackberries were good, no denying it. Time flew, and we were soon walking back to the boat, pockets dripping with succulent fruits.

The boat had gone.

That is a phrase that gives no idea of the sheer terror that seized us – only four miles down was Millerson's Weir, and the current was fast.

'God!' I was rooted. By the time my stomach had stopped trying to crawl up my throat, Jossy was gone too. I could see him, maybe two hundred yards down the bank, running.

It was the first time I had ever dialled the famous '999' call. 'Police, please,' I said. No one the other end seemed disturbed. They asked where I was, what had happened – it took a long time.

Not knowing what was going to happen, I went back to the river. There was a huge crowd on the bank, word had spread.

In the turbulent, knotting waters was the boat being thrown to and fro, in it Ted. And clutching it, pulling it to land: JOSSY! I couldn't believe my eyes. This son of a drunkard, wimp of Warlshaw – saving a lad's life less than five hundred yards from the weir.

For the second time in an hour, my stomach did acrobatics. No one had ever survived once they were in that stretch of water. It was said that the mud harboured the bones of no less than seven men.

And here was Joss, swimming against the current with a boat behind him.

His reception was immense. Mrs Ted had hysterics, there were at least four policemen and even Joss's father turned up – in a foul temper.

Joss was on the telly, too. He was there with his father, who kept saying 'Oh yesh, he'sh a fine boy,' and ruffling Joss's hair. Joss looked very uncomfortable.

And the papers. *Amazing Child Hero Saves Boy From Certain Death*, read the headlines. New-found friends flocked to the Pherit household.

But soon everything was back to normal. The short-term associates retreated into the background, and I had a chance to ask Joss what had happened. 'Why on earth did you do it, Jossy?' I asked. 'I wouldn't 'a' dared.' He looked guilty, and finally leant forward, and said, confidingly: 'Well, I'd borrowed my dad's fishing tackle, hadn't I? Couldn't let that go over the weir . . . '

Guy Burt (12)

The escapologist

They buried him under twelve tons of concrete.
It was quick setting.
They estimated that the sheer weight of the concrete would
crush his coffin-prison.
Chained in a plastic cell with no way out.
Was this to be his last
Attempt to defy the laws of nature and humanity?
'Pour the concrete!'
They gave him approximately three minutes to live,
Three minutes to escape.

Would the bonds of steel and stone defeat the new
  Houdini?
One minute passes.
They glance nervously at digital watches on executive
  wrists.
Two minutes pass.
There is no movement from the entombed life, no ripple
In the concrete.
Houdini himself nearly died in an attempt to escape from
A trial burial.
He seems to preside over this event, slowing down time,
  but
The third minute passes.
There is a murmur, they begin to notice the tombstone
already
In place at the graveside.
It seems that this is indeed to be the final escape.
A finger, wait, a hand
Rises from the grave, attached to an arm, a shoulder,
His head reaches the surface.
As they cheer, the man struggles out of the twelve foot
Prison. His grey eyes
See nothing, they are blind, plugged with concrete. His ears
Are grey and deaf.
His grey hair matches his grey hands, grey face, grey body.
He stands, staggers,
Falls to his knees in gratitude. He is a survivor.
He lives to die.
This man has proved that it is possible to escape anything.
Even death.

Clare Milner (15)

Closing of the door

God keep us safe this night,
Secure from all our fears,
May angels guard us while we sleep
Till morning light appears.
Amen.

A kiss, 'Goodnight love, sleep tight, I'll
see you in the morning. Here's Dear-Dear and
your Teddy.' Kiss; 'Goodnight.'

'Wait, *wait*,
No, *no, Auntie*, NO,
PLEASE
I never have the door shut I never have the light off
till I'm asleep, Auntie please, *please*, PLEASE –'

'WILL you be quiet.
I've never heard such a noise.
Why, you're a big boy now you go to school.
What noise, Good Heavens,
I've never heard such nonsense in all my life.
Now you just stop that,
right this minute.
What a baby, I don't know –
your father *will* be cross
when he comes home and hears
you've been *so* naughty!'

Naughty – what? who did she
mean? My Daddy never shuts the door,
he never turns my light out –

'Goodness Gracious,
will you *stop* that noise –
you'll wake your baby sister up,
she doesn't make a row like that.'

The sounds grown softer, she goes downstairs.

When they came back –
an hour or so, no more –
Mummy heard him softly crying,
picked him up and soothed it all away:
brought him peace and warmth and quiet.
He knew then
the worst night of his life was over,
tomorrow was another happy day.

A kiss, 'Don't worry, you can have your light on
all the time – as bright, as bright as any star,
as bright as anything you want. Here's Dear-Dear and
your Teddy.' Kiss; 'Goodnight.'

He's sixteen now, and still remembers every word.

God keep us safe this night.
Secure from all our fears,
May angels guard us while we sleep
Till morning light appears.
Amen.

Mick Gowar

Do you believe in ghosts?

'I'll tell you something,' said Daial to Iain. 'I believe in ghosts.'

It was Hallowe'en night and they were sitting in Daial's house – which was a thatched one – eating apples and cracking nuts which they had got earlier that evening from the people of the village. It was frosty outside and the night was very calm.

'I don't believe in ghosts,' said Iain, munching an apple. 'You've never seen a ghost, have you?'

'No,' said Daial fiercely, 'but I know people who have. My father saw a ghost at the Corner. It was a woman in a white dress.'

'I don't believe it,' said Iain. 'It was more likely a piece of paper.' And he laughed out loud. 'It was more likely a newspaper. It was the local newspaper.'

'I tell you he did,' said Daial. 'And another thing. They say that if you look between the ears of a horse you will see a ghost. I was told that by my granny.'

'Horses' ears,' said Iain laughing, munching his juicy apple. 'Horses' ears.'

Outside it was very very still, the night was, as it were, entranced under the stars.

'Come on then,' said Daial urgently, as if he had been angered by Iain's dismissive comments. 'We can go and see now. It's eleven o'clock and if there are any ghosts you might see them now. I dare you.'

'All right,' said Iain, throwing the remains of the apple into the fire. 'Come on then.'

And the two of them left the house, shutting the door carefully and noiselessly behind them and entering the calm night with its millions of stars. They could feel their shoes creaking among the frost, and there were little panes of ice on the small pools of water on the road. Daial looked very determined, his chin thrust out as if his honour had been attacked. Iain liked Daial fairly well though Daial hardly read any books and was only interested in fishing

and football. Now and again as he walked along he looked up at the sky with its vast city of stars and felt almost dizzy because of its immensity.

'That's the Plough there,' said Iain, 'do you see it? Up there.'

'Who told you that?' said Daial.

'I saw a picture of it in a book. It's shaped like a plough.'

'It's not at all,' said Daial. 'It's not shaped like a plough at all. You never saw a plough like that in your life.'

They were gradually leaving the village now, had in fact passed the last house, and Iain in spite of his earlier protestation was getting a little frightened, for he had heard stories of ghosts at the Corner before. There was one about a sailor home from the Merchant Navy who was supposed to have seen a ghost and after he had rejoined his ship he had fallen from a mast to the deck and had died instantly. People in the village mostly believed in ghosts. They believed that some people had the second sight and could see in advance the body of someone who was about to die though at that particular time he might be walking among them, looking perfectly healthy.

Daial and Iain walked on through the ghostly whiteness of the frost and it seemed to them that the night had turned much colder and also more threatening. There was no noise even of flowing water, for all the streams were locked in frost.

'It's here they see the ghosts,' said Daial in a whisper, his voice trembling a little, perhaps partly with the cold. 'If we had a horse we might see one.'

'Yes,' said Iain still trying to joke, though at the same time he also found himself whispering. 'You could ride the horse and look between its ears.'

The whole earth was a frosty globe, creaking and spectral, and the shine from it was eerie and faint.

'Can you hear anything?' said Daial who was keeping close to Iain.

'No,' said Iain. 'I can't hear anything. There's nothing. We should go back.'

'No,' Daial replied, his teeth chattering. 'W-w-e w-w-on't go back. We have to stay for a while.'

'What would you do if you saw a ghost?' said Iain.

'I would run,' said Daial, 'I would run like hell.'

'I don't know what I would do,' said Iain, and his words seemed to echo through the silent night. 'I might drop dead. Or I might . . . ' He suddenly had a terrible thought. Perhaps they were ghosts themselves and the ghost who looked like a ghost to them, might be a human being after all. What if a ghost came towards them and then walked through them smiling, and then they suddenly realized that they themselves were ghosts.

'Hey, Daial,' he said, 'what if we are . . . ' And then he stopped, for it seemed to him that Daial had turned all white in the frost, that his head and the rest of his body were white, and his legs and shoes were also a shining white. Daial was coming towards him with his mouth open, and where there had been a head there was only a bony skull, its interstices filled with snow. Daial was walking towards him, his hands outstretched, and they were bony without any skin on them. Daial was his enemy, he was a ghost who wished to destroy him, and that was why he had led him out to the Corner to the territory of the ghosts. Daial was not Daial at all, the real Daial was back in the house, and this was a ghost that had taken over Daial's body in order to entice Iain to the place where he was now. Daial was a devil, a corpse.

And suddenly Iain began to run and Daial was running after him. Iain ran crazily with frantic speed but Daial was close on his heels. He was running after him and his white body was blazing with the frost and it seemed to Iain that he was stretching his bony arms towards him. They raced along the cold white road which was so hard that their shoes left no prints on it, and Iain's heart was beating like a hammer, and then they were in the village among the ordinary lights and now they were at Daial's door.

'What happened?' said Daial panting, leaning against the door, his breath coming in huge gasps.

And Iain knew at that moment that this really was Daial, whatever had happened to the other one, and that this one would think of him as a coward for the rest of his life and tell his pals how Iain had run away. And he was even more frightened than he had been before, till he knew what he had to do.

'I saw it,' he said.

'What?' said Daial, his eyes growing round with excitement.

'I saw it,' said Iain again. 'Didn't you see it?'

'What?' said Daial. 'What did you see?'

'I saw it,' said Iain, 'but maybe you don't believe me.'

'What did you see?' said Daial. 'I believe you.'

'It was a coffin,' said Iain. 'I saw a funeral.'

'A funeral?'

'I saw a funeral,' said Iain, 'and there were people in black hats and black coats. You know?'

Daial nodded eagerly.

'And I saw them carrying a coffin,' said Iain, 'and it was all yellow, and it was coming straight for you. You didn't see it. I know you didn't see it. And I saw the coffin open and I saw the face in the coffin.'

'The face?' said Daial and his eyes were fixed on Iain's face, and Iain could hardly hear what he was saying.

'And do you know whose face it was?'

'No,' said Daial breathlessly. 'Whose face was it? Tell me, tell me.'

'It was your face,' said Iain in a high voice. 'It was your face.'

Daial paled.

'But it's all right,' said Iain. 'I saved you. If the coffin doesn't touch you you're all right. I read that in a book. That's why I ran. I knew that you would run after me. And you did. And I saved you. For the coffin would have touched you if I hadn't run.'

'Are you sure,' said Daial, in a frightened trembling voice. 'Are you sure that I'm saved?'

'Yes,' said Iain. 'I saw the edge of the coffin and it was almost touching the patch on your trousers and then I ran.'

'Gosh,' said Daial, 'that's something. You must have the second sight. It almost touched me. Gosh. Wait till I tell the boys tomorrow. You wait.' And then as if it had just occurred to him he said, 'You believe in ghosts now, don't you?'

'Yes, I believe,' said Iain.

'There you are then,' said Daial. 'Gosh. Are you sure if they don't touch you you're all right?'

'Cross my heart,' said Iain.

Iain Crichton Smith

Thinking and writing

His first flight by Liam O'Flaherty

An important part of this story is the way in which the young seagull's feelings change between the beginning of the story and the end. How would you describe his thoughts and feelings when the story begins? And at the end?

What do you learn about people from this story? (Can you, for example, think of situations in which human beings might behave and feel like this?)

Unsuspected hero by Guy Burt

This is a story that has a twist in the ending. What difference would it make to the story if the last two sentences were missed out?

Different people would probably have very different opinions of Jossy. Write three short descriptions of him – his appearance· and his character – that might have been written by:

> his father
> the newspaper reporters
> his last head teacher.

The escapologist by Clare Milner

Some people think that people like this escapologist are just plain stupid, while others admire them and think that they are both brave and talented. What is your opinion and why?

The poem tells a story full of suspense. It has a particular pattern based on the length of the lines. What is the pattern? Does it help keep up the suspense?

You can tell a story like this in many different ways. Here it is told as a poem. Write a different version of it in one of these ways:

- as a radio commentary

- as a TV interview with the escapologist *after* the escape
- as told by a close friend who has been very worried for his safety.

Closing of the door by Mick Gowar

There is another poem by Mick Gowar on page 14. If you like his poems you will find more of them in *So Far so Good*.

Like the boy in the poem, some people cannot sleep unless there is a light on near them. Others find it difficult to get to sleep if there is the slightest glimmer of light – or the slightest sound. Why do you think some people are afraid of the darkness while others are not?

Do you believe in ghosts? by Iain Crichton Smith

What do you think Daial would have done if Iain had told the truth about what he had seen?
Why did Iain tell the particular story that he did tell?
What is your opinion of the way Iain behaved?

Into orbit

In this section there are stories and poems about the future, space, the planet we live on – and one or two surprises.

Our Solar System

We made a model of the Solar System today
On our school field after lunch.
Sir chose nine of us
To be planets
And he parked the rest of the class
In the middle of the field
In a thoroughly messy bunch.
'You're the sun,' he brays,
'Big, huge; stick your arms out
In all directions
To show the sun's rays.'
The bit about sticking arms out
Really wasn't very wise
And I don't mind telling you
A few fingers and elbows
Got stuck in a few eyes.
Big Bill took a poke at Tony
And only narrowly missed him.
And altogether it looked

50

More like a shambles
Than the start of the Solar System.
The nine of us who were planets
Didn't get a lot of fun:
I was Mercury and I stood
Like a Charlie
Nearest of all to the sun,
And all the sun crowd
Blew raspberries and shouted
'This is the one we'll roast!
We're going to scorch you up, Titch,
You'll be like a black slice of toast!'
Katy was Venus and Val was Earth
And Neville Stephens was Mars,
And the sun kids shouted and
Wanted to know
Could he spare them any of his Bars.
A big gap then to Jupiter (Jayne)
And a bigger one still to Saturn,
And Sir's excited and rambling on
About the System's mighty pattern.

'Now, a walloping space to Uranus,' he bawls,
'It's quite a bike ride away from the sun.'
Ha blooming ha – at least somebody here's
Having a load of fun.
He's got two planet kids left
And Karen's moaning
About having to walk so far:
She's Neptune – I suppose Sir's
Cracking some joke about
Doing X million miles by car.
Pete's Pluto – 'The farthest flung of all,'
Says Sir,
He's put by the hedge and rests,
But soon he starts picking blackberries
And poking at old birds' nests.
'Of course,' yells Sir, 'the scale's not right
But it'll give you
A rough idea.
Now, when I blow my whistle
I want you all to start on your orbits –
Clear?'
Well, it wasn't, of course,
And most of the class, well,
Their hearts weren't really in it,
Still, Sir's O.K. so we gave it a go,
With me popping round the sun
About ten times a minute,
And Pluto on the hedge ambling round
Fit to finish his orbit next year.
We'd still have been there but
A kid came out of the school and yelled,
'The bell's gone and the school bus's here!'
Well, the Solar System
Broke up pretty fast,
And my bus money had gone from my sock
And I had to borrow.
I suppose we'll have to draw diagrams
And write about it tomorrow.

Eric Finney

The fun they had

Margie even wrote about it that night in her diary. On the page headed 17 May, 2155, she wrote, 'Today Tommy found a real book!'

It was a very old book. Margie's grandfather once said that when he was a little boy *his* grandfather told him that there was a time when all stories were printed on paper.

They turned the pages, which were yellow and crinkly, and it was awfully funny to read words that stood still instead of moving the way they were supposed to – on a screen, you know. And then, when they turned back to the page before, it had the same words on it that it had had when they read it the first time.

'Gee,' said Tommy, 'what a waste. When you're through with the book, you just throw it away, I guess. Our television screen must have had a million books on it and it's good for plenty more. I wouldn't throw *it* away.'

'Same with mine,' said Margie. She was eleven and hadn't seen as many telebooks as Tommy had. He was thirteen.

She said, 'Where did you find it?'

'In my house.' He pointed without looking, because he was busy reading. 'In the attic.'

'What's it about?'

'School.'

Margie was scornful. 'School? What's there to write about school? I hate school.' Margie always hated school, but now she hated it more than ever. The mechanical teacher had been giving her test after test in geography and she had been doing worse and worse until her mother had shaken her head sorrowfully and sent for the County Inspector.

He was a round little man with a red face and a whole box of tools with dials and wires. He smiled at her and gave her an apple, then took the teacher apart. Margie had hoped he wouldn't know how to put it together again, but he knew how all right and after an hour or so, there it was again, large and black and ugly with a big screen on which

all the lessons were shown and the questions were asked. That wasn't so bad. The part she hated most was the slot where she had to put homework and test papers. She always had to write them out in a punch code they made her learn when she was six years old, and the mechanical teacher calculated the mark in no time.

The inspector had smiled after he was finished and patted her head. He said to her mother, 'It's not the little girl's fault, Mrs Jones. I think the geography sector was geared a little too quick. Those things happen sometimes. I've slowed it up to an average ten-year level. Actually, the overall pattern of her progress is quite satisfactory.' And he patted Margie's head again.

Margie was disappointed. She had been hoping they would take the teacher away altogether. They had once taken Tommy's teacher away for nearly a month because the history sector had blanked out completely.

So she said to Tommy, 'Why would anyone write about school?'

Tommy looked at her with very superior eyes. 'Because it's not our kind of school, stupid. This is the old kind of

school that they had hundreds and hundreds of years ago.'
He added loftily, pronouncing the word carefully,
'*Centuries* ago.'

Margie was hurt. 'Well, I don't know what kind of
school they had all that time ago.' She read the book over
his shoulder for a while, then said, 'Anyway, they had a
teacher.'

'Sure they had a teacher, but it wasn't a *regular* teacher,
it was a man.'

'A man? How could a man be a teacher?'

'Well, he just told the boys and girls things and gave
them homework and asked them questions.'

'A man isn't smart enough.'

'Sure he is. My father knows as much as my teacher.'

'He can't. A man can't know as much as a teacher.'

'He knows almost as much I betcha.'

Margie wasn't prepared to dispute that. She said, 'I
wouldn't want a strange man in my house to teach me.'

Tommy screamed with laughter. 'You don't know
much, Margie. The teachers didn't live in the house. They
had a special building and all the kids went there.'

'And all the kids learned the same thing?'

'Sure, if they were the same age.'

'But my mother says a teacher has to be adjusted to fit
the mind of each boy and girl it teaches and that each kid
has to be taught differently.'

'Just the same they didn't do it that way then. If you
don't like it, you don't have to read the book.'

'I didn't say I didn't like it,' Margie said quickly. She
wanted to read about those funny schools.

They weren't even half finished when Margie's mother
called, 'Margie! School!'

Margie looked up. 'Not yet, mamma.'

'Now,' said Mrs Jones. 'And it's probably time for
Tommy, too.'

Margie said to Tommy, 'Can I read the book some more
with you after school?'

'Maybe,' he said, nonchalantly. He walked away
whistling, the dusty old book tucked beneath his arm.

Margie went into the schoolroom. It was right next to her bedroom, and the mechanical teacher was on and waiting for her. It was always on at the same time every day except Saturday and Sunday, because her mother said little girls learned better if they learned at regular hours.

The screen was lit up, and it said: 'Today's arithmetic lesson is on the addition of proper fractions. Please insert yesterday's homework in the proper slot.'

Margie did so with a sigh. She was thinking about the old schools they had when her grandfather's grandfather was a little boy. All the kids from the whole neighbour-hood came laughing and shouting in the school-yard, sitting together in the school-room, going home together at the end of the day. They learned the same things so they could help one another on the homework and talk about it.

And the teachers were people . . .

The mechanical teacher was flashing on the screen: 'When we add the fractions $\frac{1}{2}$ and $\frac{1}{4}$ —'

Margie was thinking about how the kids must have loved it in the old days. She was thinking about the fun they had.

Isaac Asimov

. . . .

(This text has been transcribed and translated, using a Titan B789000 computer, from the Alphan computer printout. This was found in the wreckage of a space-vehicle, discovered in the Himalayas, in 2080. Only a few fragments of a much longer document survived the disastrous fire which destroyed all life-forms on the vehicle.)

. . . .

Galactic Government Health Warning.
Earth is a high-risk planet,
And is to be visited
Only with the greatest caution.

Seen through a telescope,
You may think
Earth a lovely planet.
Alphan travellers are warned,
This is pure deception.
Earth is tricky,
In places, toxic,
And earth-dwellers
Are not to be trusted,
Being primitive and untamed
Members of the galaxy;
Violent polluters
Of their own biosphere.
Earth is as bizarre a planet,
As any in the universe.

How to exchange data with Earth-men

Earth-men are beginning to learn
To use computers for communication,
But much data-transfer is done
By a primitive method,
Long forgotten on Alpha-B375.
This uses a gaseous medium
To transmit a pattern
Of low-frequency vibrations,
Over a short distance.
This pattern is coded and decoded
Into a series of non-digital signals,
Which yet can carry meaning,
When received by head-organs,
Long defunct in Alphans.

You will need several megabytes
Of computer memory,
To store and decode
The patterns used,
In addition to
Complex hardware and software.

Earth-men call this system,
SPEECH.

To make matters worse,
Differing patterns are used
In different parts of Earth.
Earth-men call this system,
LANGUAGE.

Being complex, vague, and uncertain,
Many coding and decoding errors
Are produced by these systems.
Earth-men call these errors,
MISUNDERSTANDINGS.

Now you will understand
Why earth-men are forever fighting.

Further systems have been observed,
Using sustained vibrations,
At regular intervals,
With repeated patterns,
Some with a mathematical basis.
It is not known why
Earth-men use these.
At times they seem
To have a calming effect,
At other times to excite,
And cause the Earth-men
To move in strange ways,
Even to laugh or weep.
The Earth-men call these systems,
MUSIC and POETRY.

From this you will see,
What a strange planet
Earth can be.

John Cunliffe

Living fire

Zigger's granny said, 'Suppose I must get the washing in before it gets dark, oh dear me, and the lunch things still in the sink, I don't know. And it's turning so chilly you'd think it was winter. A nice fire, that's what we'll have, a real blizzy. You get the fire going, Zigger, there's a good boy, there's nothing like a fire. You'll need to get some coal in – what's that dratted cat doing on the table? Shoo, shoo! After the butter, the old devil! I know his ways. Yes, you get the coal, we'll need more coal, and then we'll have a blaze, a real blizzy . . .'

Zigger went outside to get the coal. He thought. 'It's not all that cold, but I suppose she feels it more . . . Well, she's old. Seventy. Seventy! Seven times as old as me. And old-fashioned. Washing on the line, coal fires, that big old cat.'

He was not complaining; just thinking. He liked staying with Gran. He liked seeing washing on a clothes-line instead of looping the loop in a tumble-drier. He liked the special voice Gran put on, ever so ladylike, when she answered the phone. And he liked the coal fire.

'A living fire,' she called it. And she was right.

He took the washing off the line for her, then filled the coal box. She came out, saw the washing in the wicker basket, said, 'Oh! Aren't you a thoughtful boy!' and took it in. Zigger lugged the coal box through the kitchen, said, 'Gerroff!' to Satan, the black cat, who was on the table again, eyeing the butter, and put the coal box at the side of the fireplace. He knelt in front of the fire, staring at it.

Dead. Dust and ashes. 'Well,' he said to himself, 'we'll soon fix that! Soon, you'll be alive again, with little tongues of flame darting about and smoke curling round itself and rushing up the chimney. Later, you'll be a fine old lazy, red and gold monster, crinkling and crackling, flaring and flaming; with burning caves and fiery pictures inside you . . .'

Gran came in and saw him kneeling there, staring. 'Dreaming again!' she said. 'You're awful, yes you are, oh dear me!' She was smiling, of course. 'You get that fire going, there's a love, and I'll see to the dishes, where's the dishcloth gone, oh there it is. Yes, you see to the fire, that's up to you.'

'It's up to you,' the Captain said. His voice was grave; even a little afraid. 'All up to you, Zigger. We rely on you. If you fail . . . But you won't fail, you've never failed yet.'

Zigger said nothing. He merely returned the steady gaze of the Captain's eyes. Blue-grey eyes they were, blue-grey like the spacesuit he wore. And bright as the visor of the space helmet the Captain held in the crook of his arm. A good man, a fine captain. But worried.

Zigger nodded, saluted and went to work. Already his mind had completed the list of what he would need to complete the task that lay ahead.

First, the Thermic Bombs.

He opened the Top Security locker with his Priority codecard and removed a packet. REDDIFLAME, the packet said. There was even a crude picture of a fire, topped with brightly-coloured flames. Zigger smiled sardonically. A security measure, of course. Clever camouflage. Zigger knew – who better? – what the packet really contained. Thermic bombs!

With sure, steady fingers he opened the flap of the packet, and (careful, now, very careful!) slid out the bombs. They were in a block. Each bomb had to be broken away individually. Faint lines showed the breaking points.

'Right!' he murmured. 'Here . . . we . . . go!' He applied pressure. He knew exactly how much to use. Too little – or too much for that matter – and you'd get an uneven break. An irregular fission of this sort could, it was rumoured, start a chain explosion, an uncontrolled holocaust that would range through the whole Galaxy.

With an almost inaudible *snap*, a thermic bomb separated. Perfect. A tidy, unbroken oblong. Zigger let go the breath he had been holding and thought, 'O.K. Stage One completed, but only Stage One. Now to construct the Energy Pile. Get on with it, man!'

He got on with it. Almost casually – for the risky part

was over for the moment – he tossed the thermic bomb on top of the Launching Pad. The bomb lay there, white and innocent, very brilliant against the dull lattice of special metals that formed the pad. White, harmless, almost friendly . . .

How different from what came next – the glittering black Solar Capsules! These had the power of the sun itself locked within them. They had to be handled with kid gloves.

Kid gloves . . . Yet all Mission Control had supplied was this single Hand Protector! Zigger picked it up and stared disgustedly at it. An obsolete pattern; and damaged at that. He let the thing drop and settled back on his heels to think. Ah, of course. He'd have to rely on the Remote handler: a clumsy apparatus, tricky to use even in expert hands. But Zigger was no ordinary expert.

He flexed the handler and said, 'O.K. Operational.' With the skill born of long experience, he used the muscular movements of his own right hand to manipulate the jaws at the end of the Remote handler. 'Come on, now . . . ' he said to the handler. 'Come on, come on . . . gently does it . . . ' The jaws closed, very slowly but very certainly. '*Lift!*' Zigger grated – and began lifting. It was easy when you knew how. Zigger knew how.

Again and again he repeated the actions – select, close jaws, lock on, lift, transport, position, disengage. Soon a heaped pile of solar capsules almost hid the thermic bomb. Almost, but not quite. There had to be a place left open, of course. A flame path, an ignition trail, a gap to admit the Igniter. 'Steady now,' Zigger whispered. He was actually using his naked fingertips to clear exactly the right space.

The Alien must have heard Zigger's whispered words – for it was there, beside him! It had moved on silent feet, with incredible stealth, seeking out human company.

Zigger made no move, showed no surprise. He was used to alien beings. Some flew, some scuttled, some crawled. Some even lived underground. So? So you came to terms with them. You played it cool.

This Alien was of a species that walked silently – probed fearlessly – and invaded, remorselessly, the habitats of mankind. It pushed its face closer and closer towards Zigger's. Its blank, unyielding eyes, metallic gold, stared unblinkingly into his. Zigger did not refuse the challenge. 'Well, what do you want?' he demanded, his voice hard and clear. As he spoke, he knew how meaningless his words were. Few Aliens had mastered even the simplest human speech: this species seemed deliberately to ignore it.

The Alien made its move! Its blunt, black head, driven by the full power of the splendidly muscled body, hit Zigger square on the forehead. There was no pain – just this sudden, jolting, totally unexpected impact.

Zigger rocked on his heels – recovered his balance – grated, 'You devil!' and gave back blow for blow, forehead to forehead.

The Alien knew its master. It retreated. It sat and stared, at first in silence. But then it began to make its low, rumbling sound . . .

'Where's that dratted cat?' Gran called from the kitchen.

'He's all right, Gran. He's here, with me.'

'What's he up to?'

'He's purring.'

'Well, as long as he's not at the food, *that's* all right. How are you getting on?'

'How are you getting on?' the Captain said. He was trying to sound at ease and unworried.

Zigger merely pointed a finger in reply. The Captain took in what had already been accomplished and slowly nodded his head. 'I knew I could rely on you,' he said. 'And, Zigger, as you know better than anyone, maintenance of correct temperatures is vital to the success of this operation –'

'I'll see it through, sir. Rely on me.'

'I do, I do! And when the job's done, you won't be forgotten, Zigger. Rely on me for that!' The Captain's mouth worked briefly with strong emotion; then he nodded and was gone.

Somewhere in the distance, bells shrilled. There was a definite pattern to the ringing. The Alien heard. It turned its head to the source of the sound; then looked at Zigger, a question in its eyes.

'Even if I explained,' Zigger said, 'you wouldn't understand.' The bells continued their wild clamour; then suddenly ceased. 'Perhaps,' Zigger said, 'it's better that you *don't* understand. So many complications and contradictions . . . ' The Alien stared at him with large, uncomprehending eyes. Zigger shrugged. 'All that matters to you, old chap,' he said, 'is that I complete my mission.'

He clenched his jaws and returned to his task. He checked and double-checked. Thermic bomb? Positioned and ready to go. Solar capsules? Fine — an ideal ignition pattern. That left the igniters — the triggers, the means of initiating the whole operation. *Where were they? Where were the igniters?*

For a brief instant, Zigger's heart stopped.

It was the Alien who resolved the crisis. It rose to its feet, arched the massive ridges of muscle along its spine, waved its fifth limb — and there they were! The igniters! The black bulk of the Alien had concealed them.

Gasping with relief, Zigger flung himself on the vital little container. 'Imbecile!' he hissed at the Alien. 'Don't you see — without these, we would have remained for ever in Status Standby! We would hold and hold, with the temperature constantly falling — with conditions becoming, hour by hour, minute by minute, ever more intolerable!'

He checked himself. 'What's the use of blaming *you*?' he said, in a low voice. 'You simply don't understand . . . ' The Alien blinked and stared. Zigger braced himself and got back to work.

Using the forefinger of his right hand as if it were the piston of some precision machine, he slid open the inner section of the container. He extracted a single igniter and stared at it, wondering if one would be enough. Often he had succeeded with just one igniter, but there was always the lingering doubt . . . 'Oh, get on!' he told himself. 'You're deliberately wasting time!' Time mustn't be wasted. The thing had to be done and now was the time to do it.

In the distance the bells rang once. 'Did-Dang!' they

said, and were silent. Zigger knew full well what the sound of the bells meant: the end. Time had run out.

He raised his head, straightened his shoulders and took a deep breath. Then, holding the small container in his left hand and the igniter in his right, *he struck*.

He struck – and a spark spurted, twinkled, glowed, died. He struck again and, cursing, yet again.

At last a flame flickered, dwindled, but then grew, triumphantly! It leapt outwards, always growing! Narrow-eyed, Zigger stared at the flame, willing it to grow stronger, knowing that when it did he would not have to strike again.

The flame steadied. The climactic moment had come!

Almost as if completing a sacrament, Zigger arched his body forwards, stretched out his rigid hand, and directed the flame, millimetre by millimetre, towards the flame path.

'Count down!' he muttered. 'Ten, nine, eight, seven, six, five . . .'

Gran came in. 'That was your Mum on the telephone,' she said. 'From a call-box. They don't give you much time to talk, do they? You're hardly started before you're finished, oh dear me. Anyhow, they're in the car on their way back home and they're going to pick us up here and take us out to dinner in a restaurant, isn't that grand? An evening out for you and me both! So you needn't light the fire after all.'

So Zigger didn't.

Nicholas Fisk

The waiting game

The Spymaster hung like a bauble of tinsel against a black, star-strewn sky. For an advanced war machine, and one that had cost its government eleven million dollars to build, it looked surprisingly flimsy, rather like an Art Nouveau version of a flywheel. It also looked very dead, for it had whirled in the same orbit now for around seven years without once transmitting a signal or firing its retrorockets to avoid colliding with the debris of its previous victims – spy satellites whose exploded fragments necklaced the Earth. The Spymaster, since the day of its launch, had accounted for hundreds of these simple machines as effortlessly as a swallow dealing with a swarm of gnats. It was equipped with lasers, and though these were not limitless in range they had proved quite sufficient for its numerous targets. The remains of these, from twinkling clouds of particles to quite considerable chunks the size of a human head, danced ghost-like in the wake of their silent destroyer.

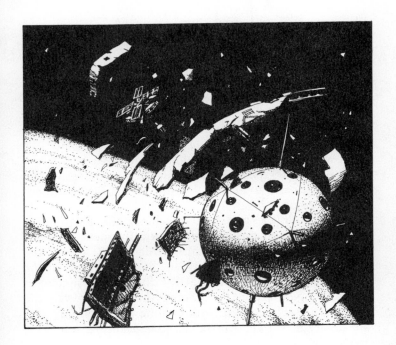

But not all of them were dead. In among this pathetic chain there was one that was not altogether defunct, still a whole unit, functioning though dormant; a tiny machine of enemy design, newer than the Spymaster, made in answer to it and deliberately miniaturized so that it could camouflage itself among its opponent's derelict trophies. It was as if some cannibal warrior had strung the skulls of the vanquished round his belt, and discovered that in the sockets of one, eyes still gleamed.

For a while the Spymaster had not even realized what was going on. It had known that transmissions were being made from time to time somewhere in its sky, and vainly checked each quadrant for the satellite which must be destroyed. It had circled the Earth like a silver hawk, searching, listening, and never caught more than the dying murmur of a report at the moment of completion. Eventually it had come to understand that it was being tricked: it knew how its enemy must be hiding. And yet the thing fell silent whenever the Spymaster swept too close;

hiding itself among the tumbling shards of all those earlier victims, small, inert, innocent. As it could not be found, it must therefore be made to give itself away.

And so for seven years, with the patience of a machine, the Spymaster had lain quiet, and would now for seventy, or seven hundred if need be, for a machine cannot lightly make a decision nor without reason change its course. Sooner or later the miniscule enemy must transmit: the Earth would speak and it would have to answer. The spy might be as wary as a mouse near a sleeping cat. But what if the mouse came to believe that the cat was dead, and not merely sleeping?

Far beneath the two rival machines the Earth hung lustrous, blue and misty, as enigmatically silent as themselves. The fierce fire storms which had swept the continents were quenched now in the rising levels of the seas, and the clouds of radioactive dust had dissipated in the thinning atmosphere. Smiling through her veil the Earth turned, cloaked in cloudy white like a virgin; and, like a virgin, sterile. Above her the deadly combatants circled.

Nothing broke the silence.

Rita Morris

Thinking and writing

Our Solar System by Eric Finney

This poem tells the story from the viewpoint of one of the children. How do you think 'Sir' thought about it? The poem gives us a few clues about what he was like. Read the poem again to form your own opinion of him. Then write *his* version of what happened in the lesson.

The fun they had by Isaac Asimov

Isaac Asimov is a very famous writer of science fiction and popular books about science. He has written a lot about robots.

We already have the technology to make the 'mechanical teacher' possible. But it would be *very* expensive. In time it will become much cheaper. What would be the advantages and disadvantages of a system of mechanical teachers as described in the story?

If we get to the stage of having mechanical teachers, what will the rest of our lives be like?

Alpha-B375 – Earth visitors' guide by John Cunliffe

This poem comes from a collection called *Standing on a Strawberry*. John Cunliffe is also well known as the author of the Postman Pat books.

This poem can be read purely for fun, but it also has some serious things to say about human beings and their life on earth. Some of them are criticisms, but not all. Read the poem again and make a list of the things it says *for* and *against* human beings.

Suppose some more of the document was found. What would it say? Write your own version of the section that deals with one of these topics:

school
sport
travel
TV.

Living fire by Nicholas Fisk

Nicholas Fisk has written a large number of science fiction stories. This one comes from a collection called *Living Fire and Other Stories*. There are more short stories in *Sweets from a Stranger*. His full-length books include:

Antigrav	Robot Revolt
Grinny	Snatched
Leadfoot	Space Hostages
Mind-benders	Time Trap
Rag, a Bone and a Hank of Hair	Trillions

If this is what Ziggy does when he is lighting a fire, what does he do when he is mending a puncture on a bike? Or running errands? Or tidying his bedroom? Or travelling to school? Make up a story about someone who turns his or her own life into an adventure as Ziggy does. (It needn't be about space travel; it might be a historical romance, or a spy story, or an adventure amongst the Mafia . . .)

The waiting game by Rita Morris

What is the Spymaster?
What is it looking for?
What has happened to Earth?
Is the story about machines or people?

Parents and children

In this section there are three stories and a poem on the theme of children learning things about their parents. Sometimes it is not a very happy experience, but for all the children it is an important part of growing up and learning about the world they live in.

Mysteries of the heart

'Come on, Sherlock, do your detective stuff and find my cheque-book for me.'

Alan's mum was always losing things and for as long as he could remember he had helped her find them. Sometimes they were silly little things like a pair of scissors or a kitchen knife but sometimes they were big things. Like the time they went on a day trip to France and she lost their passports. Everybody had gone rushing round the supermarket in a panic – even dad – but Alan had decided to run back to the café where they'd had lunch and he had found the passports under a table.

'How do you do it?' his mum always asked, smiling with relief, when he handed her something she'd lost.

He didn't really know – he just got a feeling about where to look and most of the time he was right. His dad said it must be ESP but his young sister, Janey, said it was because he was a busybody who liked poking his nose into everything. Of course, that didn't stop her asking him for help when she lost something but the funny thing was that he hardly ever managed to find things for her.

In fact it only really worked for his mum and that was probably because he hated it when she looked helpless or upset. Whenever he saw those worry lines crease up round her eyes there was a small stab in his heart and he just wanted to make everything all right for her. That was partly why he hadn't gone on at breakfast this morning. His dad's friend had rung to ask if anyone wanted to go sailing with him in his new boat and his dad had said, 'You bet. I'd love to come and so would Janey.'

As soon as he put the phone down he sort of apologized to Alan, saying that there was only enough room for three in the boat and that Janey deserved a treat because she had been ill for a couple of weeks. That was true but Alan still felt it wasn't fair just to choose her without talking about it first. He'd started to say something but he'd seen those worry lines suddenly appear round his mum's eyes so he'd forced a smile and said it was OK. The worry lines had gone so it had been worth it. But now they were back again.

'What on earth could I have done with it?' his mum was saying as she searched through her bag looking for her cheque-book. 'Come on, Sherlock – do your trick. Dad'll do his nut if I can't find it.'

'Don't be silly – dad never does his nut about anything. He just goes quiet.'

'That's what I mean. He goes all quiet and understanding and I feel such a fool. That's because I am one, I suppose.'

'You're not,' Alan said, putting his arm round her shoulder and noticing that he was as tall as she was now.

'Well, let's just say that I make more mistakes than most people.' She turned and looked him straight in the eyes.

'I'll be taller than you soon,' he said. 'Taller than dad, too. Fancy two shorties like you having a beanpole like me.'

Her eyes flicked away from his for a moment then she laughed and said. 'OK, Beanpole, can you see my cheque-book from your great height?'

'Don't worry, I'll find it,' he said.

But he didn't. He kept thinking of places – down the side of the sofa; behind the fridge; under the kitchen table – but each time he was wrong.

'It's no good, love,' his mum said, at last, 'I've got to go – the shops close early on Saturdays. I'll get some money out of the machine at the bank.'

She asked if he wanted to go with her but he said no – the cheque-book had to be somewhere in the house and he'd made up his mind he was going to find it. She grabbed a basket, put on her coat and rushed out of the house.

As soon as she'd gone he sat on the stairs and tried to concentrate: where was the cheque-book? After a moment he stood up and walked up the stairs to his parents' bedroom. He looked round the room casually and noticed that his dad had left the top off his bottle of aftershave. The bedroom always smelled strongly: a combination of his mum's perfume, his dad's aftershave and a vaguely dusty smell from the old pink carpet.

He picked up the aftershave, splashed some into his hand and then slapped it onto his face. He liked the smell of it and the slight sting on his skin. He looked in the mirror and couldn't help smiling at himself – it was silly putting on aftershave when he didn't shave yet. He peered closer: there was a definite fuzz round his chin and across his upper lip. It was strange to think that he was going to change – that he had nearly stopped being a boy and was getting ready to become a man.

In the mirror he saw the open door of his parents' wardrobe. He turned round and walked across to it. There, on the floor next to a pair of shoes, was the cheque-book. He picked it up and slipped it into his pocket. So, he was still the ace detective and he would be able to give his mum a surprise when she got home. He was about to turn away when he saw the small metal box at the back of the wardrobe, half-hidden by one of his mum's coats. He bent down and pulled it out.

It was locked.

Perhaps Janey was right – perhaps he *was* just a busybody – but he suddenly wanted to find out what was

74

inside. It was a mystery and detectives always wanted to solve mysteries. Why was it locked? No, that wasn't the question yet. Where was the key? – that was the question.

He put the metal box on the bed and looked round the room. It was like that game where you hunted for something and people told you whether you were hot or cold. So – where was the key? The wardrobe? Cold. Ice cold. Nobody would leave the key near the locked box. The chest of drawers? Much warmer. Which drawer? Top? Cold. Second? Warmer. Third? Hot.

He opened the drawer and there, in the corner, was a little jewellery-box. He lifted the lid. Two rings, a necklace and a small key. Not bad. His detective instinct was working well.

He sat on the bed and opened the box. Papers. He flicked through them. Insurance policies, deeds to the house – official documents, that was all. Nothing interesting.

Then why was his heart beating so fast? Why was all his detective instinct telling him that there was something important here?

He unfolded one of the papers. It was his parents' marriage certificate. There was his dad's name: Leonard John Lewis, and his mum's name: Susan Eva Bumstead. Thank goodness she'd married someone with a better name. He could just imagine all the boring jokes he would have had to put up with if his name had been Bumstead.

He started to re-fold the certificate then stopped when he saw the date on the bottom. He thought it must be a mistake but when he checked he saw that the same date was written in two other places. His chest tightened and a wave of heat swept up his neck to his face.

His mum and dad had only been married for ten years. They had got married two years after he was born.

It was a shock, but it wasn't terrible. It just made him want to giggle. Lots of people got married because they were going to have a baby. Some people didn't even bother to get married at all. Why had his mum and dad waited so long, though? Two whole years – nearly two and a half, actually. He did a quick calculation. That meant that his mum was already expecting Janey when they got married. They must have decided to get married because of Janey. In that case, why hadn't they bothered to get . . . ?

Another wave of heat burned his face. He dropped the paper on the bed and began searching through the box. If there was a marriage certificate there were probably birth certificates, too. Yes. Here was Janey's. Date of birth – six months after the marriage. And this one must be his. He unfolded it.

The date of birth. The place of birth. His names. His mum's names. All the details. Except that under the column headed 'Name and Surname of Father' it didn't say Leonard John Lewis.

A shiver shook his whole body. His dad was not his dad.

After the shiver a great calm filled him. His mum might be home soon. He put the papers back, locked the box and returned it to the wardrobe, making sure it was just where he'd found it. Then he straightened the cover on the bed – his mum's and Leonard John Lewis' bed. Then he put the key back in the jewellery-box and closed the drawer.

He did it all calmly but it was as if the shiver had opened up his senses wider than they had ever been before. His eyes, ears, nose, taste-buds and skin were recording everything: the pressure of the air, the patterns of light on the carpet, the touch of his mum's coat on his skin as he put the box back. They were recording everything, and he knew that he would remember this moment for the rest of his life.

Back in his own bedroom he lay on the bed and stared at the ceiling. It didn't hurt yet. It never did at first. When his dog had been killed by that lorry he hadn't cried or felt any pain until nearly two days after it happened.

He wouldn't say anything to them, not until the pain came. He wouldn't be able to bear those worry lines round his mum's eyes, or his dad's – Leonard John Lewis' – quietness, when he told them he knew. When the pain came it might be different. It might hurt so much that he would have to tell them. He wasn't as good at keeping things secret as they were.

Janey was right: he was a nosy busybody. Well, he'd

paid for it this time. The ace detective had solved a mystery and he wished he hadn't. He wished he had gone on never knowing that there was a mystery. Although, thinking about it now, he could see all those millions of tiny clues over the years: the little looks, the sentences started but never finished, the sudden changes in mood. And the bigger clues, of course: the way it had always felt like him and mum together and Janey and his ... Janey and Leonard John Lewis together. No, a real detective would have spotted the truth years before. He was still only a boy detective and he realized how many mysteries he knew nothing about. How could you live with people and not know them? How could people keep secrets hidden in their hearts for so long? And why? He had such a lot to learn. He would have to be more on his toes for the next case.

And, of course, the next case would be a real challenge – he would be trying to find a missing person. There weren't many clues; just a name on a birth certificate: Colin Mark Drake. Oh yes, there was one other detail to help the detective – there was a strong likelihood that this mysterious stranger was tall; certainly taller than Susan Eva Bumstead and Leonard John Lewis. See, he was getting better at this game already. He was learning to put two and two together.

Alan laughed and said out loud, 'They don't call me Sherlock for nothing.'

Then he turned and pressed his face into the pillow. The pain had come much earlier than he had expected. And with the pain came the tears.

Nigel Hinton

Secrets

How do you tell your eighteen-year-old daughter she's got a sister somewhere? How do you tell her you did what you've always told her not to do? How do you get her to understand the position you were in?

How do you tell your Mum you know her secret? How do you bring it out into the open? How do you tell her you're ready to listen? How do you speak to your Mum when you don't know her as a person?

For twenty-four years I've carried my secret; the knowledge that somewhere I've got another child. My husband knows but he never mentions it. Why should he? She's nothing to him. He's only got one child. Somewhere I've got another.

I've known for a year now. I've got a sister. I'm not an only child. What does she look like? Where is she? Does Mum visit her? No, she can't. Dad wouldn't let her. He wouldn't let her get involved with anyone other than family. But she is . . . sort of.

I still remember when she was born. She was perfect. She didn't cry. Not like Helen. Even though I knew I'd be leaving her soon, I loved her. She clung to me, trusted me, gazed up at me with those huge blue eyes as if to say 'Don't leave me'.

I'm leaving home in a couple of days. Going to London. Got a job there, friends, good prospects. I've got to speak with Mum though. Ask her why. Guess I know. Hard to believe even now. My Mum, once my age. She's always been around forty, cosy and warm and well, just Mum. I've never talked to her as a person though. Never asked her how she felt, what she was thinking.

I cried when I handed her over. Come to that so did the young couple who had become my daughter's new parents. Theirs were tears of happiness though. I'm sure my, no their daugher, is happy. I'm sure they're the kind of parents we are to Helen.

79

To think a year ago I never realized, never suspected. Just wandering round the attic, searching for my old Blue Jeans magazines. Never thought that that old shoe-box would contain such a secret. Just old bits and pieces, sentimental stuff: my first baby tooth; my first pair of baby shoes; a lock of hair. Then, under that pile of old letters, that old envelope. Not thinking I had tipped out its contents. Firstly my birth certificate and then a duplicate one of hers. Emma Marie, a pretty name I remember thinking as I tip-toed down the attic steps, rushed into my room, locked the door and flung myself on the bed. I had been disgusted, no shocked to be more precise. My Mum getting rid of her own child. Why? I don't know. A year later I still don't know. That's why I've got to ask her.

Helen's leaving home in a couple of days. I've got to talk to her before she goes. She has to know the truth. She's got a right to know.

Mum's downstairs. I'll go and tell her I know. Will she deny it? Can't really. Will she cry? God I hope not, can't stand tears.

She's upstairs. I'll go and tell her now while I'm ready. Be calm. Just tell the truth.

Mum's coming upstairs. Wonder what she's doing? She's coming in here. I'll tell her now. Suddenly I'm scared. Where do I start? How do I begin?

Helen looks frightened, ill, no more . . . nervous. Yes that's it but why? My God she knows. I swear she knows. She's found out. How?

It's coming. She's going to tell me what happened herself. At last! She's going to explain. It's going to be alright.

My goodness! She's smiling. She knows but she doesn't mind. She's trying to understand. It's going to work out.

'Hello Helen.'

'*Mum?*'

'Let's talk.'

Julie Harrison (13)

Going through the old photos

Me, my dad
and my brother
we were looking through the old photos.
Pictures of my dad with a broken leg
and my mum with big flappy shorts on
and me on a tricycle
when we got to one of my mum
with a baby on her knee,
and I go,
'Is that me or Brian?'
And my dad says,
'Let's have a look.
It isn't you or Brian,' he says.
'It's Alan.
He died.
He would have been
two years younger than Brian
and two years older than you.
He was a lovely baby.'

'How did he die?'
'Whooping cough.
I was away at the time.
He coughed himself to death in Connie's arms.
The terrible thing is,
it wouldn't happen today,
but it was during the war, you see,
and they didn't have the medicines.
That must be the only photo
of him we've got.'

Me and Brian
looked at the photo.
We couldn't say anything.
It was the first time we had ever heard about Alan.
For a moment I felt ashamed
like as if I had done something wrong.
I looked at the baby trying to work out
who he looked like,
I wanted to know what another brother
would have been like.
No way of saying.
And Mum looked so happy.
Of course she didn't know
when they took the photo
that he would die, did she?

Funny thing is,
though my father mentioned it every now and then
over the years,
Mum – never.
And he never said anything in front of her
about it
and we never let on that we knew.
What I've never figured out
was whether
her silence was because
she was more upset about it
than my dad –
or less.

Michael Rosen

82

From the top deck

It would have been better if we'd moved to another town, somewhere a long way off, somewhere different; a place where, if you caught the wrong bus, you'd just get lost.

Gran wanted us to move to Bedford, to be near her. Mum's been trying to get her to move to Oxford for years, to be near *us*. Gran said all her friends were *there*, and Mum said, Well, all my friends are *here*, and so we stayed, and Gran still comes over on the bus from Milton Keynes. She has to have my room and I sleep on a sofa bed downstairs. We don't have a spare room now.

East Oxford looks like a claw on the map, like a webbed foot with claws. All the buses go down the High Street, over Magdalen Bridge, but when you get to The Plain the road branches off. One claw is St Clements, which goes on to London, one is Cowley Road which goes to Cowley, surprise surprise, and the third is Iffley Road, where we used to live.

Ours was quite near The Plain, only a little way past the bus-stop opposite the school. Charles and James used to wish that we lived further up, where you could look out across the road to the running track where Roger Bannister did the first mile in under four minutes back in nineteen fifty-something. From where we lived all you could see was the boys kicking around in the playground, and where we live now you can't see anything but the backs of the houses in the next street.

Charles and James were always after my room; I wish I'd let them have it. They had a room each, when we lived in Iffley Road, but they said they wouldn't mind sharing if they could have mine because it was the biggest, after Mum and Dad's, and it had a bay window over the porch, with a seat in it. It was the window-seat they wanted. If it had been their room, I'd never have stayed on the bus, that time.

It only took about ten minutes to walk to the city centre, when we lived in Iffley Road, so if we weren't on our bikes

we usually did walk there and back. We still do, although it's further to go, now. But that Saturday it was coming up to Christmas and I was loaded with shopping, so I caught a bus home, the 43. I caught it in Queen Street, outside the Clarendon Centre. The Cowley buses stop there as well, the ones we catch now. Anyway, it was raining.

The bus was packed, everybody had more than they could carry and what seemed like six kids each, all the same size, as if they'd been born in a litter instead of one after the other. There was a fat old bat arguing with the driver about the cost of a half fare to Howard Street which was nothing to do with him really because you buy your ticket in the queue, down in the city. There was a girl with her, who was the half fare I suppose, although she looked big enough to have children of her own, blocking the gangway and chanting, 'Boring. Boring. It's only fifteen p anyway. *Boring.*' I just shoved past her and went upstairs, which I wouldn't normally do. I feel sick on buses anyway. I usually sit as near the door as I can, to be first off at my stop. I don't like buses at all, actually. I hardly ever catch them.

But this time I went upstairs. I had three carrier-bags and a shoebox under my arm, but there was only one empty seat on the lower deck, between two people with Christmas trees. One was artificial, that was OK, it was all folded up in a polythene sheath and looked like a kind of festive guided missile, but the other one was real, with lethal twigs sticking out and it was a freak tree, it was a mutant. It had two spikes at the top instead of one, a kind of prong. I didn't fancy that shoved up my nose when I sat down, so I went up. I wish I'd risked the prong.

There weren't many people on the top deck – not when I got up there – so I grabbed the nearest seat, the little one on its own at the top of the stairs. It's on the near side, isn't it always, that little seat, next to the pavement. I sat on it because I didn't want some other nutter savaging me with a Christmas tree. If I'd sat on the other side I'd have been looking out into the road. I wouldn't have seen anything. I'd have got off at the right stop.

My room had this little bay window over the porch. I

was leaning my head against the window of the bus and what I saw, as the bus came crawling up Iffley Road, from The Plain, was that the light was on in my room. The traffic was really heavy and there was a tail-back both ways. I think we must have been held up by the lights at Donnington Bridge Road, on our side, and that's miles up the hill. I was just getting all my stuff together, but not in a hurry because I could see it would be ages before we got to the bus-stop, and when I saw that light shining out of my window, I changed my mind. I thought, I bet that's the boys mucking about in my room, and I decided to stay on the bus till the next stop. Because I wanted to look in. I wanted to see what they were up to. I hoped they'd look out and see me looking in, because I'd often looked out myself when buses went past, and wondered about the people on them. It's only when I do that sort of thing, and see people in a crowd but on their own, that I realize that people *are* people, all separate and important to themselves, like me. And anyway, I thought it would give Charles and James a shock if they looked out and saw me catching them red-handed in my room.

But mainly I just wanted to look into the room because I'd never been past our house on the bus before, because we lived so near the stop. It would have been pointless to go on to the next one. If only I'd got off where I should have.

Someone rang the bell and people got out, but I didn't. I looked down at the pavement and saw one of the Christmas trees, the one with the prong, lurching about in the yellow wet light. Then the bus moved on, about a metre at a time, up the hill. The next stop is by the church, it was going to take ages to reach it, so I didn't get up, I just sat there, and I was just sitting there when the bus came level with our house. I looked into my room. There were two people in there. It wasn't the boys, it was Mum and Dad. They were talking to each other. That's what I thought they were doing at first. I thought, when I get in I'll say, 'What were you and Dad talking about in my room, just now, eh?' and they'd wonder how I knew. But the bus didn't move and I saw that they weren't talking, they were having a row. Mum must have been doing the beds because she was clutching my duvet, like she was hugging something precious, and it was half out of its green cover. I make my own bed, of course, but I'd forgotten about it with all the Christmas shopping, and I suppose she'd looked in and seen, and said lazy cow, and gone in to do it herself. If I'd done it she wouldn't have been in there when the bus went past.

Dad had his back to her but he was talking, or yelling. His fists were clenched. He was looking out of the window, but he couldn't have been seeing anything or he'd have noticed the bus and all the people on it. It was only afterwards I realized that if anybody else on the bus had been looking out of the window, they'd have seen him too, and what happened. I thought of that Agatha Christie book where a woman on a train looks out of the window and sees a woman being murdered in a train that's on the other track, only nobody else sees.

The bus didn't move and all the time I could imagine the traffic-lights red at Donnington Bridge Road. Mum wasn't saying anything but she suddenly threw the duvet down and turned round. Dad turned too, at the same minute. They were facing each other. I saw Mum say something, just one word, and her head jerked when she said it. I saw Dad shout. I saw Mum go towards him with her arm up, and then the bus did move. Someone rang the bell which I'd been meaning to do, to get off at the church. Everyone likes to be first to ring the bell. It's childish, but everyone likes to.

But by then I'd forgotten about the bell, only I'd sort of programmed myself to get off. I wasn't really thinking of anything except getting in and finding out that I hadn't really seen what I thought I'd seen, but I got all my stuff together and went downstairs. I *was* thinking, really. I was already thinking that if I'd got off at the right stop it wouldn't have happened, like it was a kind of punishment for cheating the bus company. I wasn't feeling guilty about cheating the bus company, not out of a couple of pence, but it's not true about people's minds going blank. There's always something going on in there, even if it's really daft, like this was.

I got off the bus and ran back down the hill with all the carrier-bags bumping against my legs and the sharp corner of things making dents in me. When I took my jeans off that night I couldn't think where all the bruises had come from, at first.

The light was still on in my bedroom but I couldn't see anything from down on the front path and I couldn't hear anything because of the traffic. I've got my own door key but I didn't bother looking for it, I just ran up the steps and banged on the glass panel. It was really old, that panel, all different colours, of lilies and leaves. I used to love looking at them when the sun shone in.

Someone came running down the hall and opened the door. It was Charles. He said, 'What's the emergency? Someone jump on you?' He was grinning. I thought, nothing's happened after all. I said, 'Where's Mum?'

He stopped grinning. He said, 'What's wrong? *Did* someone jump on you?'

I said, 'Oh *yerse*. There was a rapist hiding in the holly bush.' It was about a metre high, our holly bush. Even the cat couldn't hide in it. I just wondered where Mum was,' I said.

'Doing the beds I think,' said Charles. I slammed the door, so it could be heard upstairs, and we went into the kitchen. I said, 'Where's Dad?' You'd think I'd have gone up to look for myself, wouldn't you, but I didn't. I was still waiting for everything to be all right after all. Then I heard feet on the stairs and Mum called, 'Is that Chrissie back at last?' She came into the kitchen. There was a red mark across one side of her face, a really *hard* mark, it had an edge to it. Charles said, 'Coo, you had an argument with a door, Mum?' and she laughed, dead natural, and said, 'No, I was stripping Chrissie's bed and she'd left the Dictionary of Quotations under the duvet. When I started to pull the cover off it flipped up and hit me.'

'What, the cover off the dictionary?' said Charles.

'No, you nitwit. The cover off the duvet.' She patted the red mark. 'I shall have a black eye.'

I *had* left the Dictionary of Quotations on the bed. It was such a daft excuse I'd have believed it, only I knew it

88

wasn't true, and I knew she must have been working it out as she came downstairs. I knew that I was supposed to say that I was terribly sorry because it was my fault for not putting the dictionary away and making my own bed, but I didn't. I looked at Mum and I looked at Charles and I said, 'Dad hit her.'

I didn't see it happen, but I knew. Dad never hit any of us, even, but I knew and now Charles knew, too. Dad came in and then James did. It was time to get tea ready but we all stood looking at each other and wondering how to pretend nothing had happened. I wondered how often Mum and Dad had to pretend nothing was happening. I wondered what Mum would have said if I'd let her, if I hadn't stayed on the bus, if I hadn't looked through the window. We managed to go on pretending over Christmas but by the New Year it wasn't any good. Dad wasn't home on New Year's Eve. He went to live in Banbury soon afterwards and that's when we sold the house.

I'd almost forgotten how it happened – well, forgotten to remember how it happened – until the other day. We live in Leopold Street, now, off the Cowley Road, and it's on a different bus route, further away, but you still catch the bus in Queen Street and go down the High over Magdalen Bridge.

I wasn't paying attention, I was in a hurry because we were going out and I was late. I came out of the Clarendon Centre and saw the Iffley Road bus and I ran for it. The man with the ticket machine was standing by the door. I said, 'Fifteen, please,' and he gave me a ticket. You're supposed to state destination but I didn't. If I had, he'd have told me I was getting on the wrong bus, but I never realized until we got to The Plain and the bus didn't go up Cowley Road. When I saw where we were going I couldn't move. I'd managed not to go up Iffley Road since we left, but I didn't get off. I looked out of the window.

The front garden was full of bicycles. There were students living in the house. You can always tell by the bicycles. When we were finding a new house Mum wouldn't even look at the ones that had bicycles outside. The lilies had gone from the front door and there was a piece of hardboard tacked over where the glass had been. The light was on in our front room, what had been our front room, and someone had painted the walls green. There were posters up and dead spider plants on the window sill. I was glad I was downstairs and couldn't see into my bedroom. The bus went by quite quickly so I didn't have to look long. I stayed on the bus and rode all the way up to the Magdalen Arms, and then I walked home down Magdalen Road. I hadn't cheated the bus company this time because I'd paid enough for the ticket, even though I hadn't meant to. I wasn't crying but it gave me time to stop wanting to.

But I should have got off at the proper stop. If I had, I might not have remembered what happened last time, I might have forgotten everything in the end. I might have.

Jan Mark

Thinking and writing

Mysteries of the heart by Nigel Hinton

You may have read other stories by Nigel Hinton. They include:

Beaver Towers	Run to Beaver Towers
Witch's Revenge	Getting Free
Buddy	Buddy's Song
Heart of the Valley	Collision Course

'How could people keep secrets hidden in their hearts for so long? And why?' Do you think Alan's parents were wrong not to tell him about his real father?

When do you think they should have told him? Why do you think they kept it secret?

Was Alan right to think he was a nosy busybody?

What effect do you think this discovery will have in the long run on how Alan gets on with his mother and his stepfather?

There are three people in this story. Although we see it all from Alan's point of view, we also learn quite a lot about his parents. By the end of the story what impression have you formed of Alan's mother and father?

Alan prides himself on being a good detective. In what ways does he show his detective skills in the story?

Alan is much more than just an inquisitive boy: as we go through the events of the story with him, what do we learn about the way he thinks and feels?

Secrets by Julie Harrison

Julie was thirteen when she wrote this. It is about a very similar subject to the last story, but it treats it in a very different way. What ideas is Julie trying to get across? How did you feel about the mother and daughter by the end of the story? Did you think the mother should have told her daughter earlier?

How do you think the rest of the conversation continued? Think about it and then continue from where the story leaves off.

Going through the old photos by Michael Rosen

Have you got photos like these that the family sometimes goes through? If so, you will know that many such photos have stories attached to them. (Sometimes, when the photo is of you, they are stories you would prefer not to hear re-told!) Think about *your* old photos and choose one that has a story connected with it. Tell the story. (If you prefer, you can make up an imaginary photo story.)

From the top deck by Jan Mark

Jan Mark also wrote these books:

The Ennead
Handles
Under the Autumn Garden
Hairs in the Palm of the
    Hand

Feet and other Stories
Thunder and Lightnings
At the sign of the Dog and
    Rocket
Trouble Half-Way

In case you find the 'geography' of this story a bit difficult, here is a map to show you where all the places are.

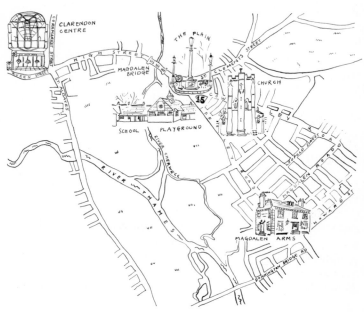

92

The feelings of the last paragraph of the story could be summed up by the words 'If only ... ' These are words that many people have said or thought at some time in their lives. Think about occasions when you have said them yourself, or heard other people say them. Now use those memories as the starting point for a story entitled *If only ...*

Thematic index

This book can be read on its own, or it can be used alongside *Oxford Secondary English Book 2* or *OSE Dimensions Book 2*. This table shows how the stories and poems in this book relate to the themes in those two books.

Oxford Secondary English 2

Unit	Story/poem
Courage	His first flight
	Unsuspected hero
	The escapologist
	Closing of the door
The days of our lives	Going through the old photos
All winter long	Living fire
Possible futures	The fun they had
	Alpha-B375 – earth visitor's guide
	The waiting game
The horror . . . . *The HORROR!*	Do you believe in ghosts?
Conflicts	Running away?
	From the top deck

OSE Dimensions 2

Unit	Story/poem
My place	Our Solar System
	Mysteries of the heart
	Secrets
	Going through the old photos
	From the top deck
Friendship	SHC
	An English lesson
What is real courage?	His first flight
	Unsuspected hero
	The escapologist
	Closing of the door